Joseph Dacre Carlyle

**Specimens of Arabian Poetry**

From the earliest time to the extinction of the Kaliphat

Joseph Dacre Carlyle

**Specimens of Arabian Poetry**

*From the earliest time to the extinction of the Kaliphat*

ISBN/EAN: 9783742812636

Manufactured in Europe, USA, Canada, Australia, Japa

Cover: Foto ©Andreas Hilbeck / pixelio.de

Manufactured and distributed by brebook publishing software (www.brebook.com)

Joseph Dacre Carlyle

**Specimens of Arabian Poetry**

# SPECIMENS

OF

# ARABIAN POETRY,

FROM THE EARLIEST TIME

TO THE EXTINCTION OF THE KHALIPHAT,

WITH

SOME ACCOUNT OF THE AUTHORS,

BY

J. D. CARLYLE, B.D. F.R.S.E.

CHANCELLOR OF CARLISLE,

AND

PROFESSOR OF ARABIC IN THE UNIVERSITY OF CAMBRIDGE.

CAMBRIDGE,

PRINTED BY JOHN BURGES PRINTER TO THE UNIVERSITY;

AND SOLD BY W. H. LUNN AND J. DEIGHTON, CAMBRIDGE; T. PAYNE & SON,
AT THE MEWS GATE; B. & J. WHITE, FLEET STREET; R. FAULDER,
NEW BOND-STREET; AND J. SEWELL, CORNHILL, LONDON;
AND FLETCHER AND COOKE, OXFORD.

MDCCXCVI.

TO THE

HONOURABLE AND RIGHT REVEREND

EDWARD VENABLES VERNON, D.D.

LORD BISHOP OF CARLISLE.

My Lord,

You will, I trust, forgive me for wishing to shelter the following trifles under your Lordship's name. When you saw them in manuscript, you were pleased to look upon their production as the innocent, yet not discreditable, amusement of a few leisure moments; and the respectable situation, in which your Lordship has since placed me, testifies that you did not consider me as less likely, from having been thus engaged, to employ my

## DEDICATION.

serious hours in more serious duties: such a testimony, allow me to say, is peculiarly valuable as coming from your Lordship, whose constant residence in your diocese, and unceasing attention to all its concerns, must ever render the attainment of your approbation one of the first wishes of your clergy.

I am,

My Lord,

Your Lordship's faithful

And most obliged servant,

J. D. CARLYLE.

# PREFACE.

THE following compositions are principally collected from the Arabian historians, by whom they have been preserved, either to elucidate some event which the author is describing, or to exemplify the genius of a poet whose life he relates. They are taken indifferently from works published, or from MSS, as the one or the other happened to fall under my perusal; and were translated at various times; either to fill up an idle moment or to dissipate the tedium of philological labour. Thus they insensibly swelled into the size of a volume.

IT was then suggested to me, that by arranging the several productions in chronological order, and affixing a short preface to each, which should contain a few anecdotes of the author, and an account of the occasion of his composition, the whole would not only afford a specimen of the writings of the principal Arabian poets, but would form a sort of history (slight indeed and imperfect, yet to an English reader perhaps not uninstructive) of Arabian poetry and literature during the most splendid period of the Mohammedan Empire.

In forming my selection of these poems, which are taken out of a much larger number of the same kind, I was chiefly guided in my choice by an appearance either of elegance or of novelty in the respective productions; but as my wish was not only to give an idea of the writings of the principal Arabian poets, but also to exemplify the different kinds of Arabian composition, I have admitted some pieces into the collection, merely upon this account, even when I could not but be conscious both of absurdity in the thought, and meanness in the execution. The generality, however, will not, I should hope, be considered as entirely destitute of poetical merit; and there are few, I trust, which can appear uninteresting to those who wish to gain an insight into the history of manners, and who love to trace the operations of the human mind in distant countries and various situations.

The English reader will perhaps be surprized to find, in these productions, so few of those lofty epithets and inflated metaphors which are generally considered as characteristic of the Oriental mode of composition; he will probably be more surprized to hear, that during the flourishing periods of Arabian literature, this bombast style was almost unknown, and that the best writers, both of poetry and prose, expressed themselves in a language as chaste and simple as that of Prior or of Addison.

TRUE taste in composition is by no means restricted to certain ages or climates, for it is no more than good sense directed to a particular object, and will be found in every country, which is arrived at that point in civilization where barbarism has ceased and fantastic refinement not yet begun.

THE writer who had obtained celebrity in the court of Bagdad during the splendor of the Khaliphat, would have smiled equally at the prosaic poetry of his European contemporaries, the Bards and Troubadours, and at the poetic prose of his own countrymen, the present Orientals. He would not easily have been tempted to describe a hero in strains such as the following, taken from one of our most popular early poets;

> " King Richard, I understonde
> Or he went out of Englonde,
> Let him make an axe for the nones
> To breake therewith the Sarasyns bones;

The heed was wrought right weel,
Therein was twenti pound of steel;
He bare a shaft that was grete and stronge.
It was fourteen foot longe,
And it was grete and stoute
One or two inches about," &c. &c.

Romance of Richard Cœur de Lion.

Nor would he have advised us, with an admired modern Persian author, " To contract the foot of tranquillity within the mantle of contentment, and not suffer the collar of patience to be torn by the hand of passion and chimera."

Anwar e Soheily, by Hassein al Kashifi.

ARABIAN literature decayed at Bagdad with the decay of the Khaliphat; and though it was transplanted thence into Egypt, and fostered at Cairo, with every attention, by the Fathemite Khaliphs and Mamluc Sultans, it could never be brought to flourish with vigour; on the appearance of the Turks, it was irrecoverably blighted.

SINCE that time, Arabic has ceased to be spoken at the courts of princes, and has yielded its place in matters of business and literature to the Turkish or Persian; but from the many valuable works which were composed in it during the existence of the Khaliphat, the Arabian tongue still continues to be considered throughout the East as the vehicle of science, and so long as Mohammedanism subsists, must always be studied as the language of religion.

As no examples taken from any Epic or Dramatic poems, are found amongst the specimens here selected, it may be supposed that the Arabians were unacquainted with the two most noble exertions of the poets' art; and should we confine our ideas of these to the common notion, viz. " a relation *in verse* of some action, either given by the Author himself, or by personages introduced upon the stage for that purpose," such a conclusion might not be erroneous; but if our definition of these kinds of poetry be not so strictly limited, we shall meet with many Arabian productions which may justly claim to be ranked amongst Epic or Dramatic poems.

The Arabian writer, who attempted either of the above-mentioned species of composition, did not consider it necessary that his work should be constructed entirely *in verse*; the descriptions, the similitudes, the reflections and many of the speeches, he expressed in numbers, but the narrative part he was satisfied with delivering in simple prose.

SEVERAL tales of the *Thousand and one nights* are written in this mixed manner, and their effect upon the passions of the reader, even under the mutilated form in which they appear to us, is pretty generally acknowledged.

FROM various parts of the old testament we may perceive that this mode of writing was practised amongst the Hebrews. In many places it is sufficiently discernible even when represented to us through the medium of a literal version; the conclusion of Genesis, where we have an account of the death of Jacob; and the xxxvi. and the three succeeding chapters of Isaiah, which contain the history of the invasion of Judea by Sennacherib and of the sickness of Hezekiah, afford examples of a mixture of different styles too apparent to be mistaken by any one.

NOR were the Orientals who used this mode of composition destitute of arguments by which they might defend it — They might allege, that such a variety in style tended to relieve weariness and awaken attention — that they were thus enabled to suit their language to the matter which they had to communicate — and as in every poem of considerable length there must be some trifling circumstances to relate, they were by this contrivance less liable to incur the ridicule which would arise from any incongruity betwixt a mean subject and a splendid diction, a ridicule from which neither the sublimity of the works of Homer nor the elegance of the Æneid could entirely exempt their respective Authors.

The greater degree of facility in compositions of this kind, tied down to no rules and subject to no restrictions but what the writer's fancy may impose, must no doubt considerably detract from the praise that is due to them; but what is lost on the one hand, is often gained on the other; as our admiration diminishes, our esteem may increase; and the performance, though less talked of, may be more read.

The difference in climate and in manners between Arabia and Europe has occasioned a smaller dissimilarity in most of the higher sorts of poetry than we could naturally expect; but in pastoral poetry, the peculiar circumstances of the inhabitants of Arabia have given them a decided superiority over other nations. The European writer of pastorals must either permit his shepherds to express themselves in the uncouth dialect which is familiar to them, or he must make them deliver their sentiments in a language unsuitable to their situation; and thus the reader is condemned to be disgusted either by the coarseness of Spencer and Theocritus; or by the unnatural refinements of Virgil and Pope.

BUT the Arabian poet laboured under no difficulties of this kind; he described only the scenes which were before his eyes, and the language of his herdsmen and cameldrivers was the genuine language used by them, by himself and by his readers; he was under no necessity of polishing away any rustic inelegancies, for he knew that the critics of Bagdad universally acknowledged the dialect of the Vallies of Yemen to be the standard of Arabian purity.

IT was in this part of the peninsula where the chief of the Arabic pastoral poems were produced; and from the cause I have stated it may be conceived that they possessed a naiveté and a raciness easy to be felt in the original language, but impossible to be transfused into any other.

As the following translations were attempted at different times and with different impressions, their execution is no doubt very unequal; in general they will, I trust, be found as literal as the nature of two languages, so little resembling each other in their structure, will admit; in some few instances I have indulged myself in a greater latitude, and have given rather an imitation than a version; in such a manner, however, I hope, as not in any place to have lost sight of the original idea of the writer.

With regard to myself, I claim no merit—The selections were made, for the most part, as chance directed me to the Authors, and the turning of them into verse demanded little effort; if I shall have succeeded in conveying to the English reader a general idea of Arabian poetry, and in rescuing it from the erroneous notions which many persons entertain respecting it, my aim will be fully answered: and I have only to hope that the trifling nature of several of the specimens may not cause the whole to appear unworthy of the Press from which they issue, and of that liberality with which my attempts have been encouraged by the Gentlemen who superintend it.

# ERRATA IN THE ARABIC.

P. 1. l. 7. for انيسيها r. انيسها. P. 1. l. 9. for مرابيع r. مرابيع. P. 2. l. 14. for تتكنسوا r. تنكنسوا. P. 3. l. 9. for الجون r. الجود. P. 3. l. 11. for وراييت r. وارايت. P. 4. l. 10. for المجامر r. المخامر. P. 14. l. ult. for فالسيل r. نالسيل. P. 21. l. 4. for ضعيف r. خعيف. P. 28. l. 8. for الولد r. مرتعد. P. 28. l. 10. for مرتعد r. مرتعد. P. 28. l. 12. for متيد r. متيد. P. 28. l. 15. for للحمام r. للحعام. P. 36. l. 11. for ولم الم r. P. 46. l. 5. for بحو r. نحو. P. 54. l. 12. after ضنوا insert غيرة. P. 58. l. 4. for للعي r. للعلي. P. 64. l. 7. for معشرة r. معشر. P. 64. l. 8. for هواي r. هراي.

---

# ERRATA IN THE ENGLISH.

P. 26. l. ult. for yield r. *gild*. P. 115. L 13. for death r. *life*. P. 120. l. 6. for poetical r. *political*. P. 126. L 18. for felluntur r. *falluntur*. P. 129. l. 14. for Romancy r. *Romanus*. P. 131. l. 12. for death r. *youth*. P. 142. L 19. for mingled streams r. *a mingled stream*. P. 148. l. 10. for beheld r. *behold*. P. 155. l. 7. for flagrance r. *fragrance*. P. 157. L 13. for exhausted r. *enchanted*. P. 178. L ult. dele *amongst*.

# I.

قـال

لبيد بن ربيعة العامري

عفت الديار محلها فمقامها
بمنّى تأبد غولها فرجامها
فمدافع الريان عري رسمها
خلقاً كما ضمن الوحي سلامها
دمنٌ تجرم بعد عهد انيسها
حججٌ خلون حلالها وحرامها
رزقت مرابيع النجوم وصابها
ودق الرواعد جودها فرهامها
من كل سارية وغاد مدجن
وعشية متجاوب ارزامها

( 2 )

نعلا فروع الابهقان واطفلت
بالجلهتين ظباوها ونعامـا
والعين ساكنة علي اطلابها
عوذا تاجل بالفضا بهامها
وجلا السيول عن الطلول كانها
زبر تجد متونها اقلامها
او رجع واشمة اسف نوورها
كنفـا تعرض نوتهن وشامها
نوقفت اسالها وكيف سوالنا
صمـا خوالد مـا يبين كلامها
عربت وكان بها الجميع فابكروا
منهـا وغودر نويهـا وثمامها
شاتتك ظعن الحي يوم تحملوا
تتكنسوا قطنـا تصر خيامها
من كل مخفوف يظل عصية
زروج عليه كلة وقرامهـا
زجلا كان نعاج توضح فوتها
وظبـا وجرة عطفـا ارامهـا
حفرت وزايلها اسراب كانمـا
اجزاع بيسة اثلمـا ورضامـا

بل مـا تذكر من نوار قد نـات
وتقطعت اسبابهـا ورمامهـا

---

## II.

قــال

الحسين الاسدي

الما علي معن وتولا لقبره
سقتك الغوادي مربعـا ثم مربعـا
فيا قبر معن انت اول حفرة
من الارض خطت للسماحة مضجعـا
ويا قبر معن كيف وريت جودة
وقد كان منه البر والبحر مترعـا
بلي قد وسعت الجود والجود ميت
ولو كان حيا ضقت حتي تصدعـا
فتي عيش في معروفه بعد موته
كما كان بعد السيل مجراه مرتعـا

---

## III.

قـال

عبد الملك الحارثي

اني لارباب القبور لغابط
بسكني سعيد بين اهل المقابر
واني لمفجوع به اذ تكاثرت
عداتي ولم اهتف سواه بناصر
فكنت كمغلوب علي نصل سيفه
وقد حز به نصل حران ثائر
اتيناه زوارا فامجدنا قري
من البث والدا الدخيل المجامر
وابنا بزرع قد نما بصدورنا
من الوجد يسقي بالدموع البوادر
ولما حضرنا لاتنسم تراثه
اصبنا عظيمات اللوي والماثر
واسمعنا بالصمت رجع جوابه
فابلغ به من ٠ ناطق لم يحاور

## IV.

قــال

ابو صاخر الهذيلي

ولو تلتقي اصداونـا بعد موتنـا
ومن دون رمسينا من الارض منكب
لظل صدي صوتي ولو كنت رمة
لصوت صدي ليلي يهتش ويطرب

---

## V.

قــال

حــاتم الطابي

اماوي ان المال غاد ورايح
ويبقي من المال الاحاديث والذكر
اماوي مــا يغني الثرا عن الفتي
ان حسرت يومــا وضاق بهـا الصدر

( 6 )

اماوي ان يصبح صداي بقفرة
من الارض لا ما لدي ولا خمر
ترى ان ما اهلكت لم يك ضرني
وان يدي مما بذلت به صفر
وقد علم الاقوام لو ان حاتما
اراد ثرا المال كان له وفر
فاني لم الو ابما لي صنيعة
فاوله زاد واخره ذخر
غنينا زمانا بالتصعلك والغنى
وكلا سقاناه يكاسيهما الدهر
فما زادنا بغيا علي ذي قرابة
غنانا ولا ازري باحسابنا الفقر

## VI.

قـال

جعفر بن علبة الحارثي

اليفي بقري سهيل حين اجلبت
علينا الولايا والعدو المباسل
فقالوا لنا ثنتان لا بد منهما
صدور رماح اشرعت او سلاسل
فقلنا لهم تلكم اذا بعد كرة
تغادر مرعى نوها متخاذل
ولم ندر ان جئنا من الموت جيفة
كم العمر بات والمدى متطاول
اذا ما ابتدرنا مازقا فرجت لنا
بايماننا بيض جلتها الصياقل
لهم صدر سيفي يوم بطحا سهيل
ولى منه ما ضمت عليه الانامل

## VII.

قــال

الفضل بن العباس

مهلا بني عمنـا مهلا موالينـا
لا تنبشوا بيننـا مـا كان مدنونـا
لا تطمعوا ان تهينونـا ونكرمكم
وان نكف الاذي عنكم وتوذونـا
مهلا بني عمنـا عن نحت اثلتنـا
سيروا رويدا كما كنتم تسيرونـا
الله يعلم انــا لا نحبكـم
ولا نلومكم ان لم تحبونـا
كل له نية في بغض صاحبه
بنعمة الله نقليكم وتقلونـا

---

## VIII.

قــال

مسكين الدارمي

وفتيان صدق لست مطلع بعضهم  
علي سر بعض غير اني جماعها  
لكل امري شعب من القلب فارع  
وموضع نجوي لا يرام اطلاعها

---

## IX.

قــال

نابغة بني جعد

اسمه قيس بن عبد الله وقيل حسن بن عبد الله ويكني ابا لبلي وهو اسن من الذبياني وطال عمره حتي ادرك ايام بني امية وهو الذي قال له النبي لا يفضض الله

فاك فمـــا سقطت له سن وفي رواية فكان
احسن الناس ثغرا اذا سقطت له سن نبتت
اخرى وعاش عشرين وماية سنة ومما يتمثل
به من شعره قوله

ولا خير في حلم اذ لم يكن له
بوادر تحمي صفوه ان تكدرا
ولا خير في جهل لم يكن له
حلم اذا اورد الامر اصدرا

---

## X.

### تسمى

### ميسون بنت بحدل

كانت ام يزيد ميسون بنت بحدل الكلبية
اقام يزيد معها بين اهلها في البادية وتعلم
الفصاحة ونظم الشعر هناك في بادية بني
كلب وكان سبب ارساله هناك مع امه ان

معاوية سمع ميسون بنت بحدل تنشد هذه الابيات وهي

للبس عبـا وتقر عيني
احب الي من لبس الشفوف
وبيت تختنق الارواح فيه
احب الي من قصر منيف
وبكر يتبع الاظعان صعب
احب الي من بغل زنوف
وكلب ينبح الاضياف دوني
احب الي من هز الدفوف
وخرق من بني عمي فقير
احب الي من علج عليف

فقال معاوية ما رضيت يا ابنة بحدل حتي جعلتني علجا عليفـا الحقي باهلك
نهضت الي بادية بني كلب ويزيد معها

———

## XI.

قــال

الخليفة يزيد بن معاوية

عاب يزيد بشرب الخمر واللعب بالكلاب
والتهاون بالدين واظهر ثلبه ونتصه للناس
باليقين المنسوبين له قيل ان والده معاوية
كان انكر عليه شرب الخمر وملازمته لتقطعه
ايامــا فقال يزيد

امن شربة من مــا كرم شربتهــا
غضبت علي الان طاب السكر
ساشرب فاغضب لا رضيت كلاهمــا
حبيب الي قلبي عقوقك والخمر

## XII.

قــال

الامام الشافعي محمد بن ادريس

ولد الشافعي سنة خمسين وماية بغزة علي الصحيح وقيل في غيرها واخذ الشافعي العلم عن مالك بن انس ومسلم بن خالد الزنجي وسفيان بن عيينة وسمع الحديث من اسماعيل بن علية وعبد الوهاب بن عبد المجيد وغيرهم قال الشافعي حفظت القران وانا ابن تسع سنين وحفظت الموطا وانا ابن عشر وقدمت علي مالك وانا ابن خمس عشرة سنة وقال رايت علي بن ابي طالب في منامي نسلم علي وصافحني وجعل خاتمه في اصبعي ونسر لي ان مصافحته لي امان من العذاب وجعله الخاتم في اصبعي انه سيبلغ اسمي ما بلغ اسم علي رضي الله

( ١٤ )

عنه في الشرق والغرب وكان الشافعي حفظا للشعر قال الاصمعي قرات ديوان الهذليين علي محمد بن ادريس الشافعي وقال ابو عثمان المازني سمعت الاصمعي يقول قرات ديوان الشنفري علي الشافعي بمكة وكان احمد بن حنبل يقول ما عرفت ناسخ الحديث حتى جالست الشافعي وتقدم الشافعي بغداد مرتين في سنة خمس وسبعين وماية ثم تقدمها مرة اخرى في سنة ثمان وسبعين وماية وناظر بشر المريسي المعتزلي ببغداد وناظر حفص الفرد بمصر فقال حفص القران مخلوق واستدل عليه نتحاربا في الكلام حتى كفره الشافعي ومما استدل به الشافعي قال الشافعي انما خلق الله الخلق بكن فاذا كانت كن مخلوقة نكان مخلوقا خلق بمخلوق وللشافعي اشعار فايقة منها من ابيات

رعت النسور بقوة جيف الفلا
ورعي الذباب الشهد وهو ضعيف

## XIII.

قــال

ابراهيم بن ادهم

في سنة احدي وستين وماية توفي ابراهيم بن ادهم بن منصور الزاهد وكان مولده ببلغ وانتقل الي الشام فاقام به مرابطا وهو من بكر بن وايل قال ابراهيم بن يسار سالت ابراهيم بن ادهم كيف كان بدو امرك حتي صرت الي الزهد قال غير ذلك اولي بك فمـا زال يلح عليه بالسوال حتي قال كان ابي من ملوك خراسان وكان قد حبب الي الصيد فبينـا انـا راكب وكلبي اذ تحركت علي الصيد فسمعت ندا من وراي يـا ابراهيم ليس لهذا خلقت ولا به امرت فوقفت مقشعرا انظر يمنة ويسرة فلم ار احدا فقلت لعن الله ابليس ثم حركت فرسي فسمعت من تربوس سرجي يـا ابراهيم ليس لهذا

خلقت ولا بهذا امرت وتلت هيهات جاني النذير من رب العالمين والله لا عصيت ربي فتوجهت الي المحلي وجيت الي بعض رعا ابي فاخذت جبته وكساه والقيت اليه ثيابي ثم سرت حتي صرت الي العراق ثم صرت الي الشام ثم قدمت الي طرسوس فاستناجرني شخص ناطورا لبستان قال فمكثت في البستان ايامـــا كثيرة كلمـــا اشتهرت اختفيت وهربت من الناس وكان ابراهيم بن ادهم ياكل من عمل يده مثل الحصاد وحفظ البساتين والعمل في الطين ومن ابياته

نرتع دنيانـــا بتمزيق ديننـــا
فلا ديننـــا يبقي ولا مـــا نرتع
فطوبي لعبد اثر الله ربه
وجاد بدنياه لمـــا يتوقع

## XIV.

قــال

اسحاق الموصلي

في تهنية الرشيد بالخلافة حين تولاهــا شعر

الم تر ان الشمس كانت مريضة
فلمــا اتي هارون اشرق نورهــا
تلبست الدنيــا جمـالا بنوره
فهارون والبهــا ويحيي وزيرهــا

---

## XV.

في قتل البرامكة

في سنة سبع وثمانين وماية كان مقتل جعفر بن يحيي وقيل السبب ان الرشيد كان لا يصبر عن جعفر ولا عن اخته عباسة بنت المهدي فزوجه بها ليحل له النظر اليهـا ونهاء عن قربها نحمله السكر علي

ان جامعها فحملت وولدت غلاما فبعث به الي مكة خوفا من الرشيد فاطلع الرشيد علي ذلك فقتل جعفر ونهب اهل بيته وقبض علي ابيه يحيي بن خالد وعلي الفضل ولده وجميع ولدهم وعمالهم ومواليهم ومن كان ينتسب اليهم وحبسهم ثم امر الرشيد براس جعفر فنصب علي الجسر وتطلعت جنبه فنصب كل تطلعة منها علي باب وكانت مدة وزارتهم للرشيد سبع عشرة سنة وكانوا في الجود والكرم الي الغاية كما هو مشهور عنهم ولم يتقدمهم من هو اكرم منهم وفيهم قال بعض الشعرا

يــا بنـي برمـك واهـا عليكــم
وعلي اوتاتكم المستقبلة
كانت الدنيــا عروسـا بكم
فهي اليوم بعدكم ارملة

## XVI.

### في طاهر بن الحسين

في سنة سبع ومايتين توفي طاهر بن
الحسين وكان في اخر جمعة صلاها قد
ترك الدعــا للمامون وتصد ان يخلعه فمات
وكان طاهر اعور ويلقب ذا اليمينين وفيه
يقول بعضهم

يــا ذا اليمينين وعين واحدة
نقصان عين ويمين زايدة

---

## XVII.

قــال

### ابو محمد

كان الواثت بالله بن المعتصم اعلم الناس
بالغنــا قال اسحاق الموصلي وكانت الالحان
العجيبة يغنيهــا ويغني بهــا شعره وشعر

غيره نقبل له يوما ها انت يا ابا
محمد فقت اهل العصر نغني شعرا ارتاح
به يومي نغني شعر

ما كنت اعلم ما في العين من حرق
حتى ينادوا بان قد جي بالسفن
قامت تودعني والدمع يغلبها
فجمجمت بعض ما قالت ولم تبن
مالت الي وضمتني لترشفني
كما يميل نسيم الريح بالغصن
واعرضت ثم قالت وهي باكية
يا ليت معرفتي اياك لم تكن

قال فخلع عليه خلعة كانت عليه وارسله
بهاية الف درهم

## XVIII.

قال

ابو تمان حبيب بن اوس الطاي

لا تنكري عطل الكريم من الغني
نالسيل حرب للمكان العالي

---

## XIX.

قال

عبد اسلام بن رغبان

ثم انت فاحثث كاسها غير صاغر
ولا تسق الا خمرها وعقارها
مشعشعة من كف ظبي كانما
تناولها من خدة فادارها

## XX.

### في ذكر المغنيين

قال ابو عكرمة البغدادي خرجت يوما الي المسجد الجامع لعلي استفيد حكمة اكتبها فمررت بباطن باب ابي عيسي ابن المتوكل فاذا علي بابه المشدود وهو احذت خلق الله بالغنا فقال اين تريد ابا عكرمة قلت المسجد الجامع لعلي استفيد حكمة اكتبها فقال ادخل بنا الي ابن ابي عيسي قلت امثل ابي عيسي في تدرته وجلالته يدخل عليه بلا اذن فقال الحاجب. اعلم امير المومنين بمكان ابي عكرمة فما لبث الاساعة حتي خرج الغلمان فحملوني خلا فدخلت الي دار ما رايت احسن بنا منها فلما دخلت عليه ونظرت الي ابي عيسي قال لي يا بغيض متي تحتشم أجلس فجلست فاتينا بطعام كثيرة فلما القضي الينا بشراب وقامت جارية تسقينا شرابا كالشعاع في زجاجه

كانبها كوكب دري فقلت اطلع الله الملك
واتم عليه نعمه ولا سلبه ما وهبه قال
فادعي ابو عيسي بالمشدود ورتيف ورايس
ولم يكن في ذلك الزمان احذق من هولا
الثلاثة بالغنا فابتدا المشدود وجعل يغني
ويقول شعر

يا دير خبة من ذات الاكيراح
من يصح عنك فاني لست بالصاحي
دع البساتين من انس وتفاح
واعدل هديت الي سفح الاكيراح
واعدل الي فتية دابت لحوميم
من العبادة لا يصحوا من الراح
وخمرة عتقت في دنها حقبا
كانها دمعة من جفن سباح

ثم سكت وجعل يغني رتيف ويقول شعر

لا تعخلن بقول اللايم اللاحي
واشرب علي الورد من شمولة الراح
كاس اذا اخدرت في حلق صاحبها
اغتني انوارها عن كل مصباح

لا زلت اسقي نذيمي ثم الثمة
والليل ملتحف ني ثوب اوشاح
نقام يحدو وقد مالت جوانبه
يا دير خبة من ذات الاكيراح

قال ثم اقبل ابو عيسي علي رايس فقال له غن نغني شعر

يا لجة الدمع هل للغمض موجوع
ام الكرا من جفون العين ممنوع
ما حيلتي ونوادي هايم دنف
بعقرب الصدغ من مولاي ملسوع
لا والذي تلفت روحي لغرته
فالقلب من فرقة الاحباب مصدوع
ما ارق العين الا حب مبتدع
ثوب الجمال علي خديه مخلوع

## XXI.
قــال
علي بن العباس المعروف بابن الرومي

رايت البنفسج في روضة
واحداته للندي شاهرة
يحاكي بها الزهر زرق العيون
واجفانــا بالبكــا فاطرة

---

## XXII.
قــال
ابن الرومي

يفتر عيسى بنفسه
وليس بياتٍ ولا خالد
ولو يستطيع لتفتيره
نفس من منخر واحد

## XXIII.

قــال

ابن الرومي

الحابس الروث في اعفاج بغلته
خونــا الي الحب من لقط العصافير

---

## XXIV.

قــال

علي بن احمد بن منصور

في سنة اثنين وثلثماية توفي علي بن احمد بن منصور الشاعر المعروف بالبسامي وكان من اعيان الشعرا كثير الهجــا هجي اباه واخوته واهل بيته وعمل في القسم بن عبيد الله وزير المعتضد

قل لابي القسم المرزي
قاتلتك الدهر بالعجايب

مات لك ابن وكان زينـــا
وعاش ذو الشين والمعايب
حياة هذا كموت هذا
فلست تخلو من المصايب

---

## XXV.

### في ميلاد

انت الذي ولدتك امك باكيـــا
والناس حولك يضحكون سرورا
ناجهد لنفسك ان تكون اذا
يبكوا في يوم موتك ضاحكا مسرورا

---

## XXVI.

قــال

ابن العلاف النهرواني

في سنة ثماني عشرة وثلثماية توفي ابو
بكر الحسن بن علي المعروف بابن العلاف
الضرير النهرواني وقد بلغ عمره ماية سنة وهو
ناظم من اثي ابر المشهورة التي منهــا

يــا هر فارقتنــا ولم تعد
وكنت منـا بمنزلة مرتعد
وكان قلبي عليه مرتعدا
وانت تنساب غير مرتعدا
تدخل برج الحمام متيدا
وتبلع الفرخ غير متيدا
صادوك غيظـا عليك وانتقموا
منك وزادوا من يصد يصد
ولم تزل للطعام مرتصدا
حتى سقيت الحمام بالرصد

( 29 )

يــا من لذيذ الغراخ اوقعه
ويحك هلا تنعت بالغدد
لا بارك الله في الطعام اذا
كان هلاك النفوس في المعد

وهي قصيدة طويلة مشهورة واختلف في سبب عملها وقيل كان له قط حقيقة وقتله الجيران فرثاه وقيل بل رثي بها ابن المعتز ولم يقدر يذكره خوفــا من المقتدر فوري بالقط وقيل بل هويت جارية لعلي بن عيسى غلامــا لابي بكر ابن العلاف المذكور فغطن بهمــا علي بن عيسى فقتلهما فقال ابو بكر مولاه هذا القصيدة وكنى عنه بالهر

## XXVII.

قــال

الشيخ محمد بن زيد المتكلم

في سنة ثلاث وعشرين وثلثماية توفي ابراهيم بن محمد بن عرفة المعروف بابن نفطويه النحوي الواسطي وله. مصنفات وهو من ولد المهلب بن ابي صفرة ولد سنة اربع واربعين وماىتىن وفيه يقول الشيخ محمد بن زيد بن علي المتكلم

من شره ان لا يرى فاسقــا
فليجتهد ان لا يرى نفطويه
احرقه الله بنصف اسمه
وصير الباقي صراخــا عليه

---

## XXVIII.

لغز في النار

واكلة باد بطن حوتها
ولا نم لها الاشجار قوت
فان اطعمتها هاجت وماجت
وان استقيتها ما تموت

---

## XXIX.

قال

الخليفة الراضي بالله

في سنة تسع وعشرين وثلثماية مات الراضي بالله ابو العباس وكانت خلافته ست سنين وعشرة ايام وكان عمره اثنين وثلثين سنة وكان اديبا شاعرا وكان سخيا يحب الادبا

والفضلاء وكان سنان بن ثابت الصابي الطبيب من جملة ندماء الراضي وجلسائه وهو اخر خليفة له شعر يدون واخر خليفة خطب كثيرا علي منبر وان كان غيره قد خطب فانه كان نادرا لا اعتبار به وكان اخر الخلفاء جلس الجلساء واخر خليفة كانت نفقته وجراياته وخزانته ومطابخه واموره علي ترتيب الخلفاء المتقدمين فمن شعره

يصفر وجهي اذا تامله
طرفي فيحمر وجهه خجلا
حتي كان الذي بوجنته
من دم قلبي اليه قد نقلا

———

## XXX.

قـال

الخليفة الراضي بالله ايضــا

كل صفو الي كدر
كل امن الي حذر
ايهــا الامن الذي
تاه في لجة الغرر
اين من كان قبلنــا
درس العين والاثر
لله در المشيب
من واعظ ينذر البشر

## XXXI.

قال

السراج الوراق

وورقــا ارتنی فوحهـا
لهــا مثل مــا لي نواد صريع
تنوح واكتم سري
ودمعي لسري لديها بديع
كاننــا تقسمنــا للهوي
فمنهــا النواح ومني الدموع

---

## XXXII.

قال

ابراهيم بن خيرة ابو اسحاق

يوم كان سحابة لبست
غمامي المصامت
حجبت بهــا شمس الضحي
بمثال اجنحة الفراخت

فالغيث يبكي فاقدها
والبرق يضحك ضحك شامت
والرعد يخطب منصصها
والجو كالمحزن ساكت

---

## XXXIII.

قال

### الامير سيف الدولة صاحب حلب

في سنة ست وخمسين وثلثماية كانت وفاة الامير سيف الدولة بن حمدان صاحب حلب وكانت مدة مملكته بحلب ثلاث وعشرين سنة وكان عمره خمس وخمسين سنة سيرته كان ملكا شجاعا كريما عالما كثير العدل والاحسان مجاهدا في سبيل الله تعالي وكان مجلسه مجمع اهل العلم وبابه قبلة الجود

ومتقصد اولي العلم والشعرا وما انفصل احد من بابه الا شاكرا لفضله وكان في بابه من الشعرا جماعة منهم المتنبي وله فيه القصايد السبع في ديوانه وابو الفرج الواوا والخالدي وابو الفرج البغــا وجماعة كبيرة وله شعر جيد من جملته قوله في جارية من بنات الملوك كان يهواهــا كثيرا فحسدها ساير خطاييه وخاف عليهــا منهن من سم فنقلها الي بعض الحصون ليحصنيــا منهن

مراتبتني العيون فيك فاشفقت
الم اخل قط من اشفاق
ورايت العدو يحيدني
فيك مجدا بانفس الاعلاق
تتمنيت ان تكوني بعيدا
والذي بيننــا من الود باقي
رب هجر يكون من خوف هجر
وفراق يكون خوف فراق

## XXXIV.

قــال

ابو الحسن الانباري

في سنة سبع وستين وثلثماية سار عضد الدولة الي العرق وكاتب الي بختيار يقول له اخرج عن هذا البلاد فاني اعطيك اي بلاد اخترت غيرها فمال بختيار الي ذلك وارسل له عضد الدولة خلعة فلبسها وسار بختيار الي نحو الشام ودخل عضد الدولة بغداد واستتر فيها وقتل وزير بختيار ابن بقيه وصلبه ورثاه ابو الحسن الانباري بقصيدته المشهورة التي منها

علوٌ في الحياة وفي الممات
بحق انت احدي المعجزات
كان الناس حولك حين قاموا
وفود نداك ايام الصلات .

مددت يديك نحوهم انتفــا      كمدهمــا اليهم بالهبات
ولمــا ضاق بطن الارض عن      ان يضم علاك من بعد الممات
اصاروا الجو قبرك واستنابوا      عن الاكفان ثوب الساقيات

---

## XXXV.

قــال

### شمس المعالي قابوس

في سنة ثلاث واربعمايـة تنل شمس المعالي قابوس بسبب تشديده علي اصحابه وعدم التجاوز عن ذنوبهم نخرجوا عن طاعته وحصروه واستدعوا ولده منوجهر فاقاموه عليهم وكان بجرجان ثم اتنف مع ابيه قابوس فانقطع في قلعة يعبد الله فلم يطب للعسكر الذين

خلعوه وعاودوا منوجهر في قتله نسكت فمتوا الي قابوس واخذوا جميع ما عنده من ملبوس وتركوه حتي مات بالبرد وكان قابوس المذكور كثير الفضايل عظيم السياسة شديد الاخذ قليل العفو وكان عالما بالنجوم وغيرها وله اشعار حسنة فمن شعره

قل للذي بصروف الدهر عيرنـــا
هل عاند الدهر الا من له خطر
امــا تري البحر تعلوا فوقه جيف
ويستقر في قعره الدرر
وفي السمــا نجوم غير ذي عدد
وليس يكسف الا الشمس والقمر

―――

## XXXVI.

في الموت

كانما العالم ضان غدت
للرعي والموت ابو جعدة
والآخر يدرك من قبله
ويترك الدنيا لمن بعده

---

## XXXVII.

قال

ابن المكرم

وليل كوجه البرتعيدي مظلم
وبرد اغانيه وطول قرونه
سريت ونومي فيه مشرد كعقل
سليمان بن فهد ودينه

( 41 )

علي اولف نيه النفاف كانه
ابو جابر في خبطه وجنونه
الي ان بدا ضو الصباح كانه
سنــا وجه ترواش وجبينه

وكان من حديث هذه الابيات ان ترواشا
جلس للشراب في ليلة شاتية وكان عنده
المذكورون وهم البرتعيدي وكان مغنيــا
لترواش وسليمان بن فهد وزيره وابو جابر
وكان حاجبــا لترواش فامر ترواش ابن الرمكرم
الشاعر ان يمدحه ويهجو المذكورين نعمل
هذه الابيات البديهية

## XXXVIII.

قال

علي بن محمد التهامي
في مات ولده صغير

حكم المنية في البرية جار
ما هذا الدنيا بدار قرار
طبعت علي كدر وانت تريدها
صفوا من الاقذا والاكدار
ومكلف الايام ضد طباعها
متطلب في الما جذوة نار
واذا رجوت المستحيل فانما
تبني الرجا علي شفير هار
فالعيش نوم والمنية يقظة
والمر بينهما خيال ساري

---

## XXXIX.

مكتوب عاشق لمعشقته

نصبت لي شرك الحب حتي اخذتني
وتركت قلبي في اواه معذب
حصلتني مثل عصفور بيد مرضعي
يذوق علاج الموت والطفل يعلب
لو للطفل ذو عقل يحن علي ما به
ولو للطير جهد يغر ويهرب

---

## XL.

قـال

ابو القاسم ابن طباطبــا الشريف

وله شعر جيد كان نقيب الطالبيين بمصر ومن اكابر روسايهــا توفي في سنة ثماني عشرة واربعماية نمن شعره

ان في نيل المني وشك الردي
وقياس القصد عند الشرف
كسراج دهنة توت له
فاذا غرتته نيه ظفي

---

## XLI.

قـــال

احمد بن يوسف المنازي

كان احمد الوزير لابي نصر احمد بن مروان الكردي صاحب ديار بكر وترسل الي القسطنطينة وكان من اعيان الفضلاء والشعرا وجمع المنازي كتبــا كثيرة واوقفها علي جامع ميافارقتين وجامع امد وكان قد اجتاز في بعض اسفاره بوادي بزاعــا

وقانـــا لفحـــة الرمضــا وان
وقاء مضاعف النبت العميم
نزلنــا دوحه فحنى علينـــا
حنو المرضعات علي الفطيم

وارشفنــا علي ظامـــا زلالا
الذ من المدامة للنديم
تروع حصاه حالية العذاري
نتلمس جانب العقد النظيم

---

## XLII.
### قـال
### قرواش صاحب الموصل

في ستة اربع واربعين واربعماية توفي
معتمد الدولة ابو منيع قرواش العقيلي الذي
كان صاحب الموصل محبوسا في تلعة
الجراحية من اعمال الموصل وقيل ان ابن
اخيه قريش بن بدران احضر عمه قرواشـا
من الحبس الي مجلسه وقتله فيه وكان
قرواش من ذوي العقل وله شعر حسن فمنه

لله در النايبات فانهـا
صدا القلوب وصيقل الاحرار
مـــا كنت الا زبرة فطبعتني
سيفــا واطلقت صرفهن عراري

## XLIII.

قـال
ابو العلا

في سنة تسع واربعين واربعماية توفي ابو العلا احمد بن سليمان المعري الاعمي وله بحو ست وثمانين سنة واختلف في عماه والصحيح انه عمي في صغره من الجدري وهو ابن ثلاث سنين وقيل ولد اعمي وكان عالما لغويا شاعرا ودخل بغداد سنة تسع وتسعين وثلثماية واقام بها سنة وسبعة اشهر واستفاد من علمايها ولم يتلمذ ابو العلا لاحد اصلا ثم عاد الي المعرة ولزم بيته وطبت الارض ذكره ونقلت عنه اشعار ومنهم

الكبر والحمد ضدان اتفاقهمـا
مثل اتفاق الشب والكبر
يجني تزايد هذا من تناقص دا
والليل ان طال غال النهار بالقصر

## XLIV.

قال

شبل الدولة في قتل نظام الملك

في سنة خمس وثمنين واربعماية قتل نظام الملك الوزير بالقرب من نهاوند قتله صبي ديلمي من الباطنية اتاه في صورة مستمنح او مستغيث فضربه بسكين كانت معه فقضى عليه وقيل ان ابتدا امر نظام الملك انه كان من ابنا الدهاقين بطوس وتعلم العربية وكان كاتبا للامير باجر صاحب بلخ وكان الامير يصادره في راس كل سنة وياخذ ما معه ويقول له قد سمنت يا حسن وهرب الي جغري بك داود وهو بمرو فدخل اليه فلما رآه اخذ بيده وسلمه الي ولده الب ارسلان وكان نظام الملك اذا دخل عليه الايمة الاكابر يقوم لهم ويجلس في مسنده وكان له شيخ فقير اذا دخل اليه

له ويجلسه في مكانه ويجلس بين يديه
فقيل له في ذلك فقال ان اوليك يقوم
اذا دخلوا علي يثنون علي بما ليس في
فيزيدني كلامهم عجبا وتيها وهذا يذكر لي
عيوب نفسي وما انا فيه من الظلم فتنكسر
نفسي لذلك فارجع عن كثير مما انا
فيه وكان مجلسه عامرا بالعلما واهل الخير
والصلاح واكثر الشعرا مراثيد فمن جيد ما
قيل قول شبل الدولة

كان الوزير نظام الملك لولوة
يتيمة صاغها الرحمن من الشرف
بدت فلم تعرف الايام تيمتها
فردها غيرة منها الي الصدف

---

## XLV.

قـالت

ولدة بنت محمد المستنفي بالله الملك الاندلس

لحاظنــا تجرحكم في الحشــا
ولحظكم يجرحنــا في الخدود
جرح بجرح فاجعلنــا ذا بذا
فمــا الذي اوجب جرح الخدود

---

## XLVI.

قــال

المعتمد بن عباد صاحب اشبيلة

في سنة ثمان وثمانين واربعماية توفي المعتمد بن عباد صاحب اشبيلة وغيرهــا من الاندلس مسجونــا باغمات واخباره مشهورة وله اشعار حسنة قال صاحب القلايد ان المعتمد

لما كان مسجوناً بأغمات دخل عليه من بنيه يوم عيد من يسلم عليه ويهنيه وفيهم بناته وعليهن أطمار كانهن كسوف وهن أقمار وأقدامهن حافية وآثار نعمتهن ثانية فقال المعتمد

فيما مضى كنت بالأعياد مسرورا
فجاك العيد في أغمات مأسورا
ترى بناتك في الأطمار جايعة
يغزلن للناس ما يملكن قطميرا
يطين في الطين والأقدام حافية
كأنها لم تطأ مسكا وكافورا
لا خد إلا تشكي الجدب ظاهره
وليس إلا مع الأنفاس ممطورا
قد كان دهرك إن كنت تأمره ممتثلا
فردك الدهر منهيا ومأمورا
من بات بعدك في ملك يسر به
فإنما بات بالأحلام مغرورا

---

## XLVII.

قــال

علي بن عبد الغني

سائر علي بن عبد الغني المتري من القيرون الي الاندلس ومدح المعتمد وغيره ثم سار الي طنجة من بر العدوة تنوفي بهـا في سنة ثمان وثمانين واربعماية وله اشعار جيدة منهـا تصيدته التي منهـا

هاروت يعلن فن السحر
الي عينيك ويسنده
واذا اغمدت اللحظ تثلت
فكيف وانت تجرده
مــا اشرك نيك القلب فلم
في نار الهجر تخلده

---

## XLVIII.

### في البطيخ

ثلاث هي في البطيخ فخر
خشونة جلده والثقل فيه
وصفرة لونه من غير علة
وفي الانسان منقصة ذاتة

---

## XLIX.

### قـــال

### المظفر الابيوردي

### في فتح بيت المقدس

ذكر ملك الفرنج القدس كان تنس قد
اتطع بيت المقدس للامير ارتت فلما توفي
صارت القدس لولديه ايلغازي وسقمان حتي
خرج عسكر خليفة مصر فاستولي علي القدس

بالامان في سنة تسع وثمانين واربعماية وبقي القدس في يد المصريين الي سنة اثنين وتسعين واربعماية وفيها تصدى الفرنج وحصروا القدس نيفا واربعين يوما وملكوه يوم الجمعة لسبع بقين من شعبان ولبث الفرنج يقتلون في المسلمين بالقدس اسبوعا وقتل من المسلمين في المسجد الاقصي ما يزيد علي سبعين الف نفس منهم جماعة كبيرة من ايمة المسلمين وعلمايهم وعبادهم وزهادهم ممن جاور في ذلك الموضع الشريف وغنموا ما لا يقع عليه الاحصا ووصل المستنفرون الي بغداد في رمضان فاجتمع اهل بغداد واستغاثوا وبكوا حتي انهم انظروا من عظم ما جري عليهم ووقع الخلف بين السلاطين السلجوتية تتمكن الفرنج من البلاد فقال المظفر الابيوردي في ذلك ابياتا منها

مزجنا دما بالدموع السواجم
فلم يبق منا عرضة للمراجم
وشر سلاح المر دمع يعتضه
اذا الحرب شبت نارها بالصوارم

وكيف تنام العين مل جفونها
علي هفوات ايقظت كل نايم
واخوتكم بالشام يضحي مقيلهم
ظهور المذاكي او بطون القشاعم
تسومهم الروم الهوان وانتم
تجرون ذيل الخفض فعل المسالم
وكم من دمـا قد ابيحـت ومن دمي
تواري حيـا حسنهـا بالمعاصم
اترضي صناديد الاعارب بالاذي
وتغضي علي ذل كماة الاعاجم
فليتهم اذ لم يذودوا حمية
عن الدين ضنوا بالمحارم

---

### L.

#### في المرأة

اقرن برايك راي غيرك واستشر
فالحق لا يخفي علي اثنين
فالمر مراة تربه وجهه
ويري تفاه بجمع مراتبين

## LI.
قـــال
جرجيس الطبيب الانطاكي
في
ابي الخير سلامة اليهودي الطبيب المصري

عليك المسكين من شومه
في بحر هلك ما له ساحل
ثلثة تدخل في دنعة
طلعته والنعش والغاسل

وكان ابو الخير قد نصب نفسه لتدريس كتب المنطق جميعها وجميع كتب الفلسفة الطبيعية والالهية وشرح بزعمه وفسر ولخص ولم يكن في تحصيله وتحقيقه هنا لك بل كان يكثر كلامه فيضل ويسرع جوابه فيزل وكان منه في عظيم ادعايه مقصوره عن ايسر ما هو يتعاطيه

___

## LII.
قـال

اسحاق بن خلف

في

رجل قصير طويل اللحية

مـا شيت داود فاستضحكت من عجب
كانه والد يمشي بمولود
مـا طول داود الا طول لحيته
نظن داود نيهـا غير موجود

---

## LIII.
قـال

مويد الدين الحسن الطغرائي

في سنة خمس عشرة وخمسماية قتل مويد الدين الحسن بن علي بن محمد الطغرائي المنشي الديلي من ولد ابي الاسود الديلي

من اهل اصفهان وكان عالما فاضلا شاعرا كاتبا منشيا خدم السلطان ملكشاه بن الب ارسلان وكان متوليا ديوان الطغر ثم بقي علي علو منزلته حتي استوزره السلطان مسعود وجري بينه وبين اخيه الحرب وانهزم مسعود واخذ الطغراي اسيرا وقتل صبرا ومن شعره قصيدة المشهورة

اعالة الراي صانتني عن الخطل
وحلية الفضل زانتني لدي العطل
مجدي اخيرا ومجدي اولا شرع
والشمس واد الضحي كالشمس في الطفل
فيم الاقامة بالزورا لاسكني
بها ولا ناقتي فيها ولا جملي
نا عن الاهل صفر الكف منفرد
كالسيف عري متناه من الخلل
فلا صديق اليه مشتكي حزني
ولا انيس اليه منتهي جذلي
طال اغترابي حتي حن راحلتي
ورحلها وقري العسالة الذبل

( 58 )

وضج من لغب نضوي وضج لما
القي ركابي ولج الركب في عذلي
اريد بسطة كف استعين بها
علي قضا حتوف للعي تبلي
والدهر يعكس امالي ويتنعني
من الغنيمة بعد الكد بالفشل
وذي شطاط كصدر الرمح معتدل
بمثله غير هياب ولا وكل
حلو الفكاهة مر الجد قد مزجت
بشدة الباس منه رقة الغزل
طردت سرح الكري عن ورد مقلته
والليل اغري سوام النوم بالمقل
والركب ميل علي الاكوار من طرب
صاح واخر من خمر الكري ثمل
نقلت ادعوك للجلي لتنصرني
وانت تخذلني في الحادث الجلل
تنام عني وعين النجم ساهرة
وتستحيل وصبغ الليل لم يحل
نيل تعين علي غي هممت به
والغي يزجر احيانا عن الفشل

اني اريد طروق الحي من اضم
وقد حماه رماة الحي من ثعل
يعمون بالبيض والسمر اللدان به
سود الغداير حمر الحلي والحلل
نسر بنا في ذمام الليل معتسفا
ونفحة الطيب تهدينا الي الحلل
فالحب حيث العدي والاسد رابضة
حول الكناس لها غاب من الاسل
لوم ناشية بالجزع قد سقيت
نصالها بمياه الغنج والكحل
قد زاد طيب احاديث الكرام بها
ما بالكرايم من جبن ومن بخل
تبيت نار الهوي منهن في كبد
حري ونار القري منهم علي القلل
يقتلن انفسا حب لا حراك بهم
وينحرون كرام الخيل والابل
يشفي لديغ العوالي في بيوتهم
بنهلة من غدير الخمر والعسل
لعل الهامة بالجزع ثانية
يدب منها نسيم البر في عللي

لا اكره الطعنة النجلاء قد شفعت
برشقة من نبال الاعين النجل
ولا اهاب الصفاح البيض تسعدني
باللمح من خلل الاستار والكلل
ولا اخل بغزلان اغازلها
ولو دهتني اسود الغيل بالغيل
حب السلامة يثني عزم صاحبه
عن المعالي ويغري المرء بالكسل
فان جنحت اليها فاتخذ نفقا
في الارض او سلما في الجو فاعتزل
ودع غمار العلى للمقدمين على
ركوبها واتنع منهن بالبلل
رضا الذليل بخفض العيش مسكنة
والعز عند رسيم الاينق الذلل
فادرأ بها في نحور البيد جافلة
معارضات مثاني اللجم بالجدل
ان العلى حدثتني وهي صادقة
فيما تحدث ان العز في النقل
لو ان في شرف المأوى بلوغ منى
لم تبرح الشمس يوما دارة الحمل

احببت بالحظ لو ناديت مستمعـــا
والحظ عني بالجهال في شغل
لعل ان قد بدا فضلي وتقصهم
لعينه نام عنهم او تنبه لي
اعلل النفس بالامال ارتبها
مــا اضيق العيش لو لا فسحة الامل
لم ارتض العيش والايام مقبلة
فكيف ارضي وقد ولت علي العجل
غالي بنفسي عرفاني بقيمتها
فصنتها عن رخيص القدر مبتذل
وعادة النصل ان يزهي بجوهره
وليس يعمل الا في يدي بطل
مــا كنت اوثر ان يمتد بي زمني
حتي اري دولة الاوغاد والسفل
تقدمتني اناس كان شوطهم
ورا خطوي اذ امشي علي مهل
هذا جزا امر اقرانه درجوا
من تبلد تتمني فسحة الاجل
وان علاني من دوني فلا عجب
لي اسوة بانحطاط الشمس عن زحل

فاصبر لها غير مختال ولا نجر
في حادث الدهر ما يغني عن الحيل
اعدي عدوك ادني من وثقت به
فحاذر الناس واصحبهم علي دخل
وانما رجل الدنيا ووحدها
من لا يعول في الدنيا علي رجل
وحسن ظنك بالايام معجزة
فظن شرا وكن منها علي وجل
غاض الوفا وفاض الغدر وانفرجت
مسافة الخلف بين القول والعمل
وشان صدقك عند الناس كذبهم
وهل يطابق معوج بمعتدل
ان كان ينفع شي في ثباتهم
علي العهود فسبت السيف للعذل
يا واردا سور عيش كله كدر
انفقت صفوك في ايامك الاول
فيم اقتحامك لج البحر تركبه
وانت يكفيك منه مصة الوشل
ملك القناعة لا يخشي عليه ولا
يحتاج فيه الي الانصار والخول

ترجو البقــا بدار لا ثبات لهــا
فهل سمعت بظل غير منتقل
ويـا خبيرا على الاسرار مطلعــا
اعتصمت في الصمت منجاة من الزلل
قد رشحوك لامر ان فطنت له
فاربــا بنفسك ان ترعي مع الهمل

---

## LIV.

قال

ابن الربيع

في

الشباب

عريت من الشباب وكنت غصنــا
كمــا يعرى من الورق القضيب
ونحت على الشباب بدمع عيني
نمــا نفع البكا ولا النحيب
الا ليت الشباب يعود يومــا
فان اخبره بمــا فعل المشيب

---

## LV.
قــال

### ابو علي المهندس

في سنة ثلثين وخمسماية كان ابو علي المهندس المصري موجودا بمصر تيمــا بعلم الهندسة وكان ناضلا فيه وفي الادب وله شعر يلوح عليه الهندسة فمن شعره

تنقسم قلبي في محبة معشرة
بكل فتى منهم هواي منوط
كان نوادي مركز وهم له
محيط واهواي لديه خطوط

---

## LVI.

قـــال
يحيي بن سلامة بن الحسن بميافارقين
في
مدح الخمر

وخليع بت اعذله
ويرى عذلي من العبث
قلت ان الخمر مخبثة
قال حاشاها من الخبث
قلت فالارمان يتبعها
قال طيب العيش في الرمث
قلت منها الغشي قال اجل
شربت مخرج الخبث
وساسلوها قلت متي
قال عند الكون في الجدث

## LVII.

قــال

### الخليفة المقتفي لامر الله

في سنة خمس وخمسين وخمسماية توني الخليفة المقتفي لامر الله وكانت خلافته اربعـا وعشرين سنة وكانت الخطبة مستمرة له ببغداد فقوي امر الخليفة بالعراق وقامت حشمة الدولة العباسية ورجعت الي احسن ما كانت عليه وكان المقتفي لامر الله فضلا حسن السيرة وله شعر حسن ومنه

قالت احبك قلت كاذبة
عزي بذا من ليس ينتقد
لو قلت لي اشناك قلت اجل
الشيخ ليس يحب احد

## LVIII.

قــال

ابن التلميذ

كان في وسط المائة السادسة من الاطبــا المشار اليهم في الاناث ثلثة افاضل معــا من ثلث ململك كل منهم هبة الله اسمــا ومعني من النصاري واليهود والمسلمين هبة الله بن التلميذ وهبة الله بن ململا ابو البركات وهبة الله بن الحسين الاصفهاني وامـا هبة الله ابن التلميذ الطبيب النصراني البغدادي نفاضل زمانه وعالم اوانه خدم الخلفــا من بني العباس وتقدم في خدمتهم وارتفعت مكانته لديهم وكان موئقــا في المباشرة والمعالجة عالمـا بقوانين هذه الصناعة عمر طويلا وعاش نبيلا جليلا وكان شيخــا بهي المنظر حسن الروا عذب المجتني والمجتبي لطيف الروح ظريف الشخص بعيد الهم عالي

( 68 )

الهمة ذكي الخاطر مصيب الفكر حازم الراي وله في نظم الشعر كلمات راقية رائقة شائقة شايقة تعرب عن لطانة طبعه ومن شعره

كانت بلهنية الشبيبة سكرة
فصحوت واستانفت سيرة مجمل
وتعدت ارتقب الغنـــا كراكب
عرف المحل فبات دون المنزل

وكان ابن التلميذ يحضر عند المقتفي كل اسبوع مرة فيجلسه لكبر سنة وتوفي في سنة ستين وخمسماية وقد قارب الماية وذهنه بحاله وساله ابنه قبل ان يموت بساعة مـــا تشتهي قال ان اشتهي

## LIX.

قال

كمال الدين بن النبيـة المصري

في سنة اثني عشر وستمـاية توفي الامير ابو الحسن علي بن الخليفة الناصر لدين الله وكان الخليفة يحبه حبـا شديد وقد رشحه لولاية العهد بعده وكان رحمه الله كثير الصدقة كريمـا كثير المعروف حسن المسيرة محبوبـا الخواص والعوام فحزن عليه الخليفه حزنـا لم يسمع بمثله ولمـا توفي اخرج نهارا ومشي جميع الناس بين يدي تابوته ولمـا دخل التابوت اغلقت الابواب وسمع الناس الصراخ العظيم من داخل التربة فيقال ان ذلك كان صوت الخليفة ودامت عليه المنـاحات في اقطار بغداد ليلا ونهارا ايامـا فلم يبق في بغداد محلة الا وفيهـا النوح ولم يبق امراة الا واظهرت الحزن الشديد

ولم يسمع ببغداد مثل ذلك في قديم الزمان ولا حديثه ولما سمعت الملوك بموته جلسوا في العزالة لابسين شعار الحزن خدمة الخليفة ورثته الشعرا فاكثروا وفيهن رثاء القاضي كمال الدين بن النبيهة المصري بقصيدة ومنها

الناس للموت كخيل الطراد
فسابق السابق منها جواد
والموت نقاد علي كفه
جواهر يختار منها الجياد
والعمر كالظل ولا بد ان يزول
ذلك الظل بعد امتداد
والله لا يدعي الي داره
الا من استصلح من ذي العباد

―――――

## LX.

### محروز عاشقة ومعشوق

زارني محبوب قلبي في الغلس
قولت اجلس انه حتي جلس
قولت يــا قلبي عيني كل المدام
زورتني في الليل لم خفت العيس
قال لم خفت ولاكن الهوي
قد اخذ الروح مني والنفس

# I.

## AN
## ELEGY
### BY
### LEBID BEN RABIAT ALAMARY.

*THE* author of this poem was a native of Yeman. He was cotemporary with Mohammed, and already celebrated as a poet when the prophet began to promulgate his doctrines. Lebid for a while united with the other Arabian wits, in ridiculing the new faith; but at length, about the sixth year of the Hejra, he declared himself a convert.

The cause of his conversion, as related by several writers, appears not inconsistent with his poetical character.

It was customary at that time, amongst the poets in Arabia, to affix to the portal of the temple of Mecca any composition which they thought possessed superior excellence, as a sort of challenge; and whoever accepted the challenge, placed his own production near his antagonist's, by which means the public were enabled to examine and decide upon the merits of each.

Lebid having written a moral poem which was greatly admired, affixed it, according to the prevailing custom, to the gate of the Caaba; for some time no person attempted to rival a composition which had obtained such universal approbation; but at length Mohammed produced the chapter of the Koran entitled Becret, and exhibited his pretended revelation upon the gate of the Temple, by the side of Lebid's poem. Lebid was one of the foremost to read his opponent's work,. he had not however perused many verses before he exclaimed, " No one could write these words without the inspiration of God," and immediately embraced Mohammedanism.

The passage which operated so powerfully upon Lebid's mind being certainly one of the most beautiful in the Koran, I venture to subjoin it: " There is nothing doubtful in this book: it is a direction to the pious who believe in the mysteries of faith, who observe-the appointed times of prayer, who distribute alms out of what we have bestowed upon them, who believe in the revelation which hath been sent down to thee, and in that which hath been sent down unto the prophets before thee, and who have firm assurance in the life to come: these are directed by their Lord, and they shall prosper. As for the unbelievers, whether thou admonish them or do not admonish them, they will not believe; God hath sealed up their hearts and their hearing; a dimness covereth their sight, and they shall suffer a grievous punishment. There are some who say we believe in God and the last day, but in reality are not believers, they seek to deceive God and those who do believe; but they deceive themselves only, and are not sensible thereof.— They are like unto one who kindleth a fire, and when it hath enlightened all around him he shuts his eyes; God taketh away their light, and leaveth them in darkness; they shall not see; they are deaf, dumb and blind, therefore will they not repent.

Or like a stormy cloud from heaven fraught with darkness, thunder and lightning; they put their fingers in their ears, because of the noise of the thunder, for fear of death; God encompasseth the infidels; the lightning wanteth but little to take away their sight; so often as it enlighteneth them they walk therein, but when the darkness cometh on them they stand still."

From the moment of Lebid's professing himself a convert to Islamism, he became one of its most zealous advocates. He now renounced all prophane poetry, and resolving to consecrate his talents to the service of religion, employed his pen, from this time, either upon subjects of piety, or in answering the sarcastic pieces which Amriolkais and the other Arabian poets were continually pouring forth. By this means he rendered himself extremely serviceable to Mohammed, and was always treated by him with the utmost distinction.

Lebid fixed his abode in the city of Cufa, where he died at a very advanced age. His last words are still preserved, and it must be confessed they breathe more the spirit of a wit than that of a devotee; they were as follows:

وجدت جديد الموت غير لذيذ

"I am going to enjoy the novelty of death, but it is a novelty by no means agreeable."

This elegy, as is evident from its nature, must have been written previous to Lebid's change of religion. Its subject is one that must be ever interesting to a feeling mind — the return of a person, after a long absence, to the place where he had spent his early years — it is in fact an Arabian Deserted Village.

*I am sensible that many of its beauties can be very inadequately represented in a translation, and that many passages which were considered as beauties by the author and his countrymen, will no longer appear such to an European critic; but still I shall hope this production of Lebid must give pleasure to any person of true taste, by its picturesque descriptions, appropriate images, and simple delineation of pastoral manners.*

*The learned reader will perceive that the MS. I have made use of (which belongs to the public library at Cambridge) differs in some few places from the text given by Sir W. Jones.*

---

THOSE dear abodes which once contain'd the fair,
   Amidst MITATA's wilds I seek in vain,
Nor towers, nor tents, nor cottages are there,
   But scatter'd ruins and a silent plain.

The proud canals that once RAYANA grac'd,
   Their course neglected and their waters gone,
Among the level'd sands are dimly trac'd,
   Like moss-grown letters on a mouldering stone.

RAYANA say, how many a tedious year
   Its hallow'd circle o'er our heads hath roll'd,
Since to my vows thy tender maids gave ear,
   And fondly listen'd to the tale I told?

How oft, since then, the star of spring, that pours
   A never failing stream, hath drench'd thy head?
How oft, the summer cloud in copious showers
   Or gentle drops its genial influence shed?

How oft, since then, the hovering mist of morn
   Hath caus'd thy locks with glittering gems to glow?
How oft hath eve her dewy treasures borne
   To fall responsive to the breeze below?

The matted thistles, bending to the gale,
   Now clothe those meadows once with verdure gay;
Amidst the windings of that lonely vale
   The teeming Antelope and Ostrich stray:

The large ey'd mother of the herd, that flies
   Man's noisy haunts, here finds a sure retreat,
Here tends her clustering young, till age supplies
   Strength to their limbs and swiftness to their feet.

Save where the swelling stream hath swept those walls,
   And giv'n their deep foundations to the light
(As the retouching pencil that recalls
   A long-lost picture to the raptur'd sight)

Save where the rains have wash'd the gather'd sand
   And bared the scanty fragments to our view
(As the \*dust sprinkled on a punctur'd hand
   Bids the faint tints resume their azure hue)

---

\* It is a custom with the Arabian women, in order to give the veins of their hands and arms a more brilliant appearance, to make slight punctures along them, and to rub into the incisions a blue powder, which they renew occasionally as it happens to wear out.

No mossy record of those once lov'd seats
    Points out the mansion to enquiring eyes;
No tottering wall, in ecchoing sounds, repeats
    Our mournful queſtions and our bursting sighs.

Yet midst those ruin'd heaps, that naked plain,
    Can faithful memory former scenes restore,
Recall the busy throng, the jocund train,
    And picture all that charm'd us there before.

Ne'er shall my heart the fatal morn forget
    That bore the fair ones from these seats so dear—
I see, I see the crouding litters yet,
    And yet the tent-poles rattle in my ear.

I see the maids with timid steps ascend,
    The streamers wave in all their painted pride,
The floating curtains every fold extend,
    And vainly strive the charms within to hide.

What graceful forms those envious folds enclose!
    What melting glances thro' those curtains play!
Sure Weira's Antelopes, or Tudah's Roes
    Thro' yonder veils their sportive young survey.

The band mov'd on—to trace their steps I strove,
    I saw them urge the camel's hastening flight,
Till the white \* vapor, like a rising grove,
    Snatch'd them for ever from my aching sight.

---

\* The vapor here alluded to, called by the Arabians *Serab*, is not unlike in appearance (and probably proceeding from a similar cause) to those white mists which we often see hovering over the surface of a river in a summer's evening after a hot day. They are very frequent in the sultry plains of Arabia, and when seen at a distance, resemble an expanded lake; but upon a nearer approach, the thirsty traveller perceives his deception. Hence the *Serab* in Arabian poetry is a common emblem of disappointed expectation.

This word occurs in Isaiah xxxv. 7.

היה הישרב לאגם

which is rendered by our translators, " And the parched ground shall become a pool." But in a prophecy consisting of promises for the confirming of happiness and the fulfilling of hope, perhaps we may translate the word שרב with as much propriety, according to its Arabic acceptation: " And the sultry vapor shall become a real lake."

Nor since that morn have I NAWARA seen,
 The bands are burst which held us once so fast,
Memory but tells me that such things have been,
 And sad Reflection adds that they are past.

## II.

ON THE

# TOMB OF MANO,

BY

## HASSAN ALASADY.

*THE simile at the conclusion of this little piece will appear elegant to every reader, but to an inhabitant of the east, where vegetation and fertility are in many places almost entirely dependent upon the overflowing of the rivers, it must have been peculiarly striking.*

FRIENDS of my heart, who share my fighs!
Go seek the turf where MANO lies,
And woo the dewy clouds of spring,
To sweep it with prolific wing.

Within that cell, beneath that heap,
Friendship and Truth and Honour sleep.
Beneficence, that us'd to clasp
The world within her ample grasp,
There rests entomb'd — of thought bereft —
For were one conscious atom left
'Twould yearn new blessings to display,
Burst from the grave, and seek the day.

But tho' in dust thy relics lie,
Thy virtues, MANO, ne'er shall die;
Tho' Nile's full stream be seen no more,
That spread his waves from shore to shore,
Still in the verdure of the plain
His vivifying smiles remain.

## III.

### ON THE
# TOMB OF SAYID,
### BY
## ABD ALMALEC ALHARITHY.

*ABD ALMALEC* was a native of *Arabia Felix*. I am unacquainted with the precise time when he flourished, but as this production is taken out of the Hamasa, *(a miscellaneous collection, made in the second century of the Hejra, of such poems as were then thought to be ancient)* it is most probable that our author was anterior to Mohammedanism.

The figure in the last stanza is undoubtedly somewhat bold, but we have many in our own language almost equally so; and while we admire the "*darkness visible*" of Milton, we ought not to find fault with the "*speaking silence*" of our Arabian poet.

BLEST are the tenants of the tomb!
   With envy I their lot survey;
For SAYID shares the solemn gloom,
   And mingles with their mouldering clay.


Dear youth! I'm doom'd thy loss to mourn
   When gathering ills around combine;
And whither now shall MALEC turn,
   Where look for any help but thine?


At this dread moment when the foe
   My life with rage insatiate seeks,
In vain I strive to ward the blow,
   My buckler falls, my sabre breaks.


Upon thy grassy tomb I knelt,
   And sought from pain a short relief—
Th' attempt was vain—I only felt
   Intenser pangs and livelier grief.

The bud of woe no more represt,
    Fed by the tears that drench'd it there,
Shot forth and fill'd my labouring breast
    Ready to blossom in despair.

But tho' of SAYID I'm bereft,
    From whom the stream of bounty came,
SAYID a nobler meed has left —
    Th' exhaustless heritage of fame.

Tho' mute the lips on which I hung,
    Their silence speaks more loud to me
Than any voice from mortal tongue,
    " What SAYID was let MALEC be."

## IV.

ON THE

## DEATH OF HIS MISTRESS,

BY

## ABU SAHET ALHEDHILY.

*THE* sentiment contained in this production determines its antiquity. It was the opinion of the pagan *Arabs*, that upon the death of any person, a bird, by them called Manah, issued from his brain, which haunted the sepulchre of the deceased, uttering a lamentable scream. This notion is evidently alluded to in Job xxi. 32.

הוּא לִקְבָרוֹת יוּבָל
וְעַל־גָּדִישׁ יִשְׁקוֹד

 "He shall be brought to the grave,
 And shall watch upon the rais'd up heap."

Along with several other superstitions, prevalent amongst Arabians, a belief in the Manah is expressly forbidden by the Koran.

Dost thou wonder that I flew
Charm'd to meet my LEILA's view?
Dost thou wonder that I hung
Raptur'd on my LEILA's tongue?—
If her ghost's funereal screech
Thro' the earth my grave should reach,
On that voice I lov'd so well
My transported ghost would dwell:
If in death I can descry
Where my LEILA's relics lie,
SAHER's dust will flit away,
There to join his LEILA's clay.

## V.

## ON AVARICE,

### BY HATEM TAI.

HATEM TAI was an Arabian chief, who lived a short time prior to the promulgation of Mohammedanism. He has been so much celebrated through the East for his generosity, that even to this day the greatest encomium which can be given to a generous man, is to say that he is as liberal as Hatem.

Hatem was also a poet; but his talents were principally exerted in recommending his favourite virtue. An Arabian author quoted by Pococke (*Spec. Hist. Arab.*) thus emphatically describes this author's character.

يشبه شعره جوده ,ويصدق قوله فعله

"His poems expressed the charms of beneficence, and his practice evinced that he wrote from the heart."

The instances of Hatem's generosity as related by Oriental historians are innumerable; I select one or two, as they afford a lively picture of Arabian manners.

The Emperor of Constantinople having heard much of Hatem's liberality, resolved to make trial of it. For this purpose he dispatched a person from his court, to request a particular horse which he knew the Arabian prince valued above all his other possessions. The officer arrived at Hatem's abode in a dark tempestuous night, at a season when all the horses were at pasture in the meadows. He was received in a manner suitable to the dignity of the imperial envoy, and treated that night with the utmost hospitality. The next day the officer delivered to Hatem his message from the emperor: Hatem seemed concerned— "If," said he, "you had yesterday apprized me of your errand, I should instantly have complied with the Emperor's request, but the horse he asks is now no more; being surprized by your sudden arrival, and having nothing else to regale you with, I ordered him to be killed and served up to you last night for supper\*." Hatem immediately ordered the finest horses to be brought, and begged the

---

\* The Arabians prefer the flesh of horses to any other food.

ambassador to present them to his master. The prince could not but admire this mark of Hatem's generosity, and owned that he truly merited the title of the most liberal among men.

It was the fate of Hatem to give umbrage to other monarchs. Numan, king of Yeman, conceived a violent jealousy against him on account of his reputation, and thinking it easier to destroy than surpass him, the envious prince commissioned one of his sycophants to rid him of his rival. The courtier hastened to the desert where the Arabs were encamped. Discovering their tents at a distance, he reflected he had never seen Hatem, and was contriving means to obtain a knowledge of his person, without exposing himself to suspicion. As he advanced, deep in meditation, he was accosted by a man of an amiable figure, who invited him to his tent: he accepted the invitation, and was charmed with the politeness of his reception. After a splendid repast, he offered to take leave, but the Arab requested him to prolong his visit; "Generous stranger," answered the officer, "I am confounded by your civilities, but an affair of the utmost importance obliges me to depart." "Might it be possible for you," replied the Arab, "to communicate to me this affair, which seems so much to interest you? You are a stranger in this place — If I can be of any assistance to you, freely command me."

The courtier resolved to avail himself of the offer of his host, and accordingly imparted to him the commission he had received from Numan: "But how" continued he, "shall I, who have never seen Hatem, execute my orders? Bring me to the knowledge of him, and add this to your other favours." "I have promised you my service," answered the Arab. "Behold I am a slave to my word." "Strike," said he, " uncovering his bosom, spill the blood of Hatem, and may my death gratify the wish of your prince, and procure you the reward you hope for. But the moments are precious—defer not the execution of your king's command, and depart with all possible expedition: the darkness will aid your escape from the revenge of my friends; if tomorrow you be found here, you are inevitably undone."

These words were a thunderbolt to the courtier. Struck with a sense of his crime and the magnanimity of Hatem, he fell down on his knees, exclaiming, "God forbid that I should lay a sacrilegious hand upon you! Nothing shall ever urge me to such a baseness." At these words he quitted the tent, and took the road again to Yeman.

The cruel monarch, at the sight of his favourite, demanding the head of Hatem, the officer gave him a faithful relation of what had passed. Numan in astonishment cried out, "It is with justice, O Hatem, that the world reveres you as a kind of divinity. Men instigated by a *sentiment of generosity may bestow their whole fortune, but to sacrifice life is an action above humanity."*

*After the decease of Hatem, the Arabs, over whom he presided, refused to embrace Islamism; for this disobedience, Mohammed condemned them all to death, except the daughter of Hatem, whom he spared on account of her father's memory. This generous woman, seeing the executioners ready to perform the cruel command, threw herself at the Prophet's feet, and conjured him either to take away her life, or pardon her countrymen. Mohammed, moved with such nobleness of sentiment, revoked the decree he had pronounced, and for the sake of Hatem's daughter, granted pardon to the whole tribe.*

---

How frail are riches and their joys?
Morn builds the heap which eve destroys;
Yet can they leave one sure delight —
The thought that we've employ'd them right.


What bliss can wealth afford to me
When life's last solemn hour I see,
When MAVIA's sympathizing sighs
Will but augment my agonies?

Can hoarded gold dispel the gloom
That death must shed around the tomb?
Or cheer the ghost which hovers there,
And fills with shrieks the desert air?

What boots it, MAVIA, in the grave,
Whether I lov'd to waste or save?
The hand that millions now can grasp,
In death no more than mine shall clasp.

Were I ambitious to behold
Increasing stores of treasur'd gold,
Each tribe that roves the desert knows
I might be wealthy if I chose:

But other joys can gold impart,
Far other wishes warm my heart—
Ne'er shall I strive to swell the heap,
Till want and woe have ceas'd to weep.

With brow unalter'd I can see
The hour of wealth or poverty:
I've drunk from both the cups of fate,
Nor this could sink, nor that elate.

With fortune blest, I ne'er was found
To look with scorn on those around;
Nor for the loss of paultry ore,
Shall HATEM seem to HATEM poor.

## VI.

ON THE

# BATTLE OF SABLA,

BY

## JAAFER BEN ALBA.

---

*THIS poem and the following, are both taken from the* Hamasa; *and afford curious instances of the animosity which prevailed amongst the several Arabian clans, and of the rancour with which they pursued each other, when once at variance.*

*The rapid progress of Mohammed was no doubt greatly owing to these continual feuds; finding the tribes disunited, and unable to form any confederacy to oppose him, he attacked them separately, and thus easily reduced them all under his subjection.*

*The antitheses contained in the second and last stanza of this poem are much admired by the Arabian commentators.*

Sabla, thou saw'st th' exulting foe
    In fancied triumphs crown'd;
Thou heard'st their frantic females throw
    These galling taunts around:

" Make now your *choice* — the terms we give,
    Desponding victims, hear;
These fetters on your *hands* receive,
    Or in your *hearts* the spear."

" And is the conflict o'er," we cried,
    " And lie we at your feet?
And dare you vauntingly decide
    The fortune we must meet?

A brighter day we soon shall see,
    Tho' now the prospect lowers,
And conquest, peace and liberty
    Shall yield our future hours."

The foe advanc'd: — in firm array
  We rush'd o'er SABLA's sands,
And the red sabre mark'd our way
  Amidst their yielding bands.

Then, as they writh'd in death's cold grasp,
  We cried, " Our *choice* is made,
These *hands* the sabre's hilt shall clasp,
  Your *hearts* shall have the blade."

## VII.

VERSES ADDRESSED TO A KINDRED TRIBE,
AT VARIANCE WITH THE ONE TO WHICH
THE POET BELONGED,

BY

ALFADHEL IBN ALABAS.

WHY thus to passion give the rein?
   Why seek your kindred tribe to wrong?
Why strive to drag to light again
   The fatal feud entomb'd so long?

Think not, if fury ye display,
   But equal fury we can deal;
Hope not, if wrong'd, but we repay
   Revenge for every wrong we feel.

Why thus to passion give the rein?
  Why seek the robe of peace to tear?
Rash youths desist, your course restrain,
  Or dread the vengeance which ye dare.

Yet friendship we nor ask from foes,
  Nor favour e'er shall hope to prove,
We lov'd you not, great ALLAH knows,
  Nor blam'd you that ye could not love.

To each are different feelings given,
  This slights, and that regards his brother;
'Tis ours to live — thanks to kind heaven —
  Hating and hated by each other.

## VIII.

ON

## HIS FRIENDS,

BY

MESKIN ALDARAMY.

---

*THIS little piece is likewise from the Hamasa. Shultens has given a translation of it, but by not preserving accurately the metaphor in the sesond line, he seems entirely to have lost the beauty of the thought. His version is as follows:*

> "Viri mihi sodales sincere juncti quorum alteri non impertio
> Arcanum alterius; *me solo ejusdem participe.*
> Eorum cuique, suus mihi in corde vacat sinus;
> Locusque secreti cujus inaccessa introspectio."

The word جماع affords a key to the whole; and I am sufficiently justified in rendering it as I have done by the authority of Taurizi, who in his Commentary upon this passage expressly says

الجماع اسم لما يجمع به الشي كنظام

i. e. "*The word* جماع *means that which connects other things together, as the cord upon which pearls are strung.*" Indeed, without this interpretation, nothing could be more flat than our poet's verses, the whole merit of them consisting in the use of expressions at the same time applicable to the string of a necklace, and to a person who enjoyed the confidence of his friends.

---

WITH conscious pride I view the band
Of faithful friends that round me stand,
With pride exult that I alone
Can join these scatter'd gems in one:
   For they're a wreath of pearls, and I
   The silken cord on which they lie.

'Tis mine their inmost souls to see,
Unlock'd is every heart to me,
To me they cling, on me they rest,
And I've a place in every breast:
    For they're a wreath of pearls, and I
    The silken cord on which they lie.

# IX.

## ON

## TEMPER,

### BY

### NABEGAT BENI JAID.

---

*THERE* have been several Arabian poets of the name of *Nabegat*: the author of these verses was descended from the family of *Jaid*. As he died in the 40<sup>th</sup>. year of the Hejra, aged one hundred and twenty, he must have been fourscore at the promulgation of Islamism; he however declared himself an early convert to the new faith.

The Arabian historians give us a curious instance of *Mohammed's* affection for him; *Nabegat* being one day introduced to the prophet, was received by him with a salutation usual enough amongst the Arabians, " May God preserve thy mouth." This benediction, proceeding from lips so sacred, had such an effect, that in an instant the *poet's teeth, which were loosened by his great age, became firm in his head, and continued sound and beautiful as long as he lived.*

*The Mohammedan doctors however are much divided in opinion upon the important point, whether Nabegat actually retained all his original teeth, or whether having lost them, he only got a new set.*

---

YES, LEILA, I swore, by the fire of thine eyes,
   I ne'er could a sweetness unvaried endure;
The bubbles of spirit, that sparkling arise,
   Forbid life to stagnate, and render it pure.

But yet, my dear maid, tho' thy spirit's my pride,
   I'd wish for some sweetness to temper the bowl;
If life be ne'er suffer'd to rest or subside,
   It may not be vapid, but won't it be foul?

## X.

### THE

# SONG OF MAISUNA.

MAISUNA *was a daughter of the tribe of Calab; a tribe, according to Abulfeda, remarkable both for the purity of dialect spoken in it, and for the number of poets it had produced. She was married, whilst very young, to the Khaliph Mowiah. But this exalted situation by no means suited the disposition of Maisuna, and amidst all the pomp and splendor of Damascus, she languished for the simple pleasures of her native desert.*

*These feelings gave birth to the following simple stanzas, which she took the greatest delight in singing, whenever she could find an opportunity to indulge her melancholy in private. She was unfortunately overheard one day by Mowiah, who was of course not a little offended with such a discovery of his wife's sentiments; and as a punishment* for her fault, he ordered her to retire from court. Maisuna immediately obeyed, and taking her infant son Yezid with her, returned to Yeman: nor did she revisit Damascus till after the death of Mowiah, when Yezid ascended the throne.

Mowiah was the fifth Khaliph in succession from Mohammed, and the founder of the Ommiad dynasty. He shewed a violent opposition at first to the new religion, but having professed himself a convert, he was received into great favour by the prophet, and advanced to the highest dignities by the succeeding Khaliphs, Abubecr, Omar, and Othman, the last of whom appointed him governour of Egypt.

Upon the murder of Othman, Mowiah determined to revenge his death, and accordingly declared an irreconcileable enmity to the house of Ali, by whose suggestions he considered the crime to have been perpetrated.

The consequence of this was a long and bloody war between the Alides and Mowiah, which at length terminated in favour of the latter. But though, during the contest, Mowiah gave innumerable proofs of valour and abilities, he was indebted for his ultimate success more to the moderation of his competitor Hassan, the son of Ali, than to his own conduct; for this virtuous prince having beheld with horror the effusion of so much Moslem blood, resolved to put a stop to it, by giving up his own pretensions to the throne; this resolution he executed in the 40th. year of the Hejra, and upon his abdication, Mowiah was acknowledged throughout the empire Commander of the faithful.

Mowiah displayed as many virtues when in possession of the Khaliphat as he had shewn talents in acquiring it, and after a glorious reign of nineteen years died at Damascus universally regretted.

The last public speech he made to his people is still preserved: " I am like corn that is to be reaped," said the dying monarch, " I have governed you till we are weary of one another; I am superior to all my successors, as my predecessors were superior to me; God desires to approach all who desire to approach him; O God, I love to meet thee, do thou love to meet me!"

---

THE russet suit of camel's hair,
    With spirits light and eye serene,
Is dearer to my bosom far
    Than all the trappings of a queen.

The humble tent and murmuring breeze
　That whistles thro' its fluttering walls,
My unaspiring fancy please
　Better than towers and splendid halls.

Th' attendant colts that bounding fly
　And frolic by the litter's side,
Are dearer in MAISUNA's eye
　Than gorgeous mules in all their pride.

The watch dog's voice that bays whene'er
　A stranger seek's his master's cot,
Sounds sweeter in MAISUNA's ear
　Than yonder trumpet's long-drawn note.

The rustic youth unspoil'd by art,
　Son of my kindred, poor but free,
Will ever to MAISUNA's heart
　Be dearer, pamper'd fool, than thee.

## XI.

### VERSES OF YEZID TO HIS FATHER MOWIAH, WHO REPROACHED HIM FOR DRUNKENNESS.

*YEZID* succeeded *Mowiah* in the Khaliphat A. H. 60; and in most respects shewed himself to be of a very different disposition from his predecessor.

He was naturally cruel, avaricious, and debauched; but instead of concealing his vices from the eyes of his subjects, he seemed to make a parade of those actions which he knew no good Mussulman could look upon without horror; he drank wine in public, he caressed his dogs, and was waited upon by his eunuchs in sight of the whole court.

Such a conduct, particularly when contrasted with the piety of former Khaliphs, with reason gave great scandal to the Mohammedan world; and accordingly we find the short reign of *Yezid* perpetually disturbed with tumults and insurrections.

This prince, notwithstanding the many crimes and follies he was guilty of, inherited his mother *Maisuna's* taste *for poetry.* Many *of his compositions upon different occasions are transmitted to us by Arabian historians: I have selected the following one as a specimen both of his profligacy and wit.*

---

MUST then my failings from the shaft
    Of anger ne'er escape?
And dost thou storm because I've quaff'd
    The water of the grape?

That I can thus from wine be driv'n
    Thou surely ne'er canst think —
Another reason thou hast giv'n
    Why I resolve to drink.

'Twas sweet the flowing cup to seize,
    'Tis sweet thy rage to see;
So first I drink myself to please,
    And next — to anger thee.

# XII.

## ON

# FATALISM,

### BY THE

## IMAM SHAFAY MOHAMMED BEN IDRIS.

*SHAFAY, the founder of one of the four orthodox sects into which the Mohammedans are divided, was a disciple of Malek Ben Ans, and the master to Ahmed Ebn Hanbal; each of whom, like himself, founded a sect which is still denominated from the name of its author.*

*The fourth sect is that of Abou Hanifah. This differs in tenets considerably from the three others, for whilst the Malekites, the Shafaites, and the Hanbalites are invariably bigotted to tradition in their interpretations of the Koran, the Hanifites consider themselves as at liberty in any difficulty to make use of their own reason.*

Shafay (as quoted by Abulfeda) gives the following account of his education and studies: "At nine years of age, I could repeat the Koran; at ten, I was master of some of the easier commentaries upon that holy book; at fifteen, I began to attend the lectures of Malek Ben Ans. It was then," continues he," that I had a vision, in which I beheld the prophet Ali Ebn Abou Taleb; he approached, and saluted me, and taking a ring from his finger, put it upon mine; and I have been assured, by those who are most conversant in the interpretation of these matters, that his salutation conveyed a promise of eternal happiness to me, and his delivery of the ring was an indication that my fame should be as extensive as his own."

Abou Yacoub relates a curious account of a disputation held at Bagdad, between Shafay and a person of the name of Hafs. The subject of their controversy was one upon which the Mohammedan theologians are to this day much divided, viz. Whether the Koran was created or eternal. Hafs maintained the former opinion, and Shafay the latter. In order to understand Shafay's reasoning, we must remark that the creation of the world is described in the Koran in these words قال كن وكان "God said be, and it was;" and hence it is agreed on all sides, that the universe was called into existence by the operation of the word be.

Shafay argued thus; "God created all things by be:" to this Hafs assented. "You affirm," continued Shafay, "that the Koran was created, and consequently that the word be, which is part of it, was created likewise:" Hafs did not deny this proposition. "Then all things, according to you," said Shafay, "were created by a created being; an impiety too gross to be uttered."

The audience were compleatly convinced by Shafay's logic, and his unfortunate antagonist was sentenced to be punished as an heretic.

The reputation Shafay acquired was not entirely the consequence of his theological writings; he published many poems, which have been much admired. The following specimen seems intended to recommend the doctrine of fatalism, a doctrine which has always been favoured by the orthodox Mohammedans.

---

NOT always wealth, not always force
    A splendid destiny commands;
The lordly vulture gnaws the corse
    That rots upon yon barren sands.

Nor want, nor weakness still conspires
    To bind us to a sordid state;
The fly that with a touch expires
    Sips honey from the royal plate.

# XIII.

TO THE

# KHALIPH HAROUN ALRASHID,

UPON HIS UNDERTAKING A PILGRIMAGE
TO MECCA,

BY

# IBRAHIM BEN ADHAM.

*IBRAHIM BEN ADHAM was a hermit of Syria, equally celebrated for his talents and piety. He was son to a prince of Khorassan, and born about the $97^{th}$. year of the Hejra.*

*The reason of his betaking himself to a religious life is thus related by Ibrahim Ben Yesar, from the holy man's own mouth. " I once requested him," says this author, " to inform me by what means he arrived at his exalted sanctity, and by what motives he was first induced to take leave of the world.*

*" For a while he continued silent, but upon my repeatedly urging him, he answered, that being one day eagerly en-*

gaged in the chase, he was surprized with hearing a voice behind him utter these words; Ibrahim! it was not for this purpose thou wert created. *He immediately stopped his horse, and turned about to see from whence the voice came, but discovering no one near, he fancied it to be an illusion, and returned to his sport. In a short time he heard the same words pronounced still more loudly,* Ibrahim! it was not for this purpose thou wert created. *He now no longer doubted the reality of the admonition, and falling down in a transport of devotion, cried out,* " It is the Lord who speaks, his servant will obey." *Immediately he desisted from his amusement, and changing cloaths with an attendant, bade adieu to Khorassan, took the road towards Syria, and from thenceforward devoted himself entirely to a life of piety and labour."*

Ben Adham performed the stated pilgrimage to Mecca without companions, and without having provided any necessaries for his journey: he obliged himself also to make eleven hundred genuflexions in every mile, by which means twelve years elapsed before he compleated his pilgrimage.

As he was returning from Mecca he met the Khaliph Haroun Alrashid, who was going thither, accompanied by a magnificent train; and it was upon this occasion that he addressed the following verses to the Commander of the faithful, as a reproach for his ostentatious devotion.

Religion's gems can ne'er adorn
The flimsy robe by pleasure worn;
Its feeble texture soon would tear,
And give those jewels to the air.

Thrice happy they who seek th' abode
Of peace and pleasure, in their God!
Who spurn the world, its joys despise,
And grasp at bliss beyond the skies.

## XIV.

### UPON THE INAUGURATION OF HAROUN ALRASHID, AND THE APPOINTMENT OF YAHIA TO BE HIS VIZIR,

BY

### ISAAC ALMOUSELY.

*ISAAC ALMOUSELY is considered by the Orientals as the most celebrated musician that ever flourished in the world.*

*He was born in Persia; but having resided almost entirely at Mousel, he is generally supposed to have been a native of that place.*

*Mahadi, the father of Haroun Alrashid, having accidentally heard Almousely sing one of his compositions, accompanied by a lute, was so charmed with the performance, that he carried him to Bagdad, and appointed him principal musician to the court; an office which Almousely filled with universal applause during the reign of five successive Khaliphs of the house of Abbas, viz. Mahadi, Hadi, Haroun, Amin and Mamoun.*

This period may be considered as the Augustan age of Arabian literature. The monarchs themselves loved and cultivated the sciences, the ministers followed their example, and men of genius flocked to the court of Bagdad from all parts of the world with an assurance of receiving those honors and rewards which their abilities merited. The empire of the Khaliphs was at this time one of the most powerful that has ever existed; it extended in Asia from the gulph of Persia and the confines of Tartary, to the Mediterranean and the Indian seas, and comprehended all the habitable part of Africa, from the isthmus of Suez to the Atlantic ocean.

Haroun Alrashid, whose inauguration is commemorated in the following verses, was the fifth of the Abbasside Khaliphs, and the second son of Mahadi. He succeeded to the throne upon the demise of his elder brother Hadi, in the 170th. year of the Hejra.

Haroun had been treated with such harshness by his brother, that the people, whose favourite he was, began to be apprehensive for his safety. The account of Hadi's death was therefore received with joy, and Haronn mounted the throne amidst the universal acclamations of his subjects.

As so many historians have written the life of Haroun, it is unnesessary to enter upon it here. He died at Bagdad after a glorious reign of twenty-three years.

Haroun, who was passionately fond of music, could not but be charmed with the talents of Almousely. At every party of amusement given by the Khaliph, Almousely made one; and he is represented, like another Timotheus, to have been able at pleasure, by the touches of his lute, to raise or depress the passions of his master.

Ebn Khalican relates the following remarkable instance of the effect of his musical powers upon the Khaliph: Alrashid having quarelled with his favourite mistress Meridah, left her in a rage, and refused to see her again. The lady was in despair, and knew not in what manner to bring about a reconciliation. In the mean time the vizer Jaafer, who had always been a friend to Meridah, sent for Almousely, and giving him a song, composed for the purpose, requested him to perform it before the Khaliph with all the pathos he was master of. Almousely obeyed; and such were the powers of his execution, that Haroun immediately bidding adieu to his anger, rushed into the presence of Meridah, and taking all the blame of the quarrel upon himself, intreated his mistress to forgive his indiscretion, and bury what was past in an eternal oblivion.

The historian adds (for such must always be the catastrophe of an Eastern story when it terminates happily) that the lady, overjoyed with this sudden alteration in the Khaliph's disposition, ordered ten thousand dishems to be *given to Jaafer*, and as much to *Almousely*; while *Haroun* on his part, not less pleased with their reconciliation than the lady, doubled the present to each.

*A mutilated copy of this composition of Almousely is preserved by Elmacin, Pag.* 112; *the one I have inserted is taken from the Mostatraf, an Arabian miscellany in prose and verse, published by Mohammed Ben Ahmed about the year of the Hejra* 800 — *It has not yet been printed.*

---

TH' affrighted sun ere while had fled,
 And hid his radiant face in night;
A cheerless gloom the world o'erspread —
 But HAROUN came, and all was bright.

Again the sun shoots forth his rays,
 Nature is deck'd in beauty's robe —
For mighty HAROUN's sceptre sways,
 And YAHIA's arm sustains the globe.

## XV.

### UPON THE
### RUIN OF THE BARMECIDES.

*THE family of Barmec was one of the most illustrious in the East. They were descended from the ancient kings of Persia, and possessed immense property in various countries; they derived still more consequence from the favour which they enjoyed at the court of Bagdad, where for many years they filled the highest offices of the state with universal approbation.*

*The first of this family who distinguished himself at Bagdad was Yahia Ben Khaled, a person endowed with every virtue and talent that could render a character compleat. He had four sons, Fadhel, Jaafer, Mohammed and Musa, none of whom shewed themselves unworthy of such a father. Yahia was chosen by the Khaliph Mahadi to be governour to his son Haroun Alrashid, and when Haroun succeeded to the Khaliphat, he appointed Yahia* to be his grand vizir, an event alluded to in the preceding composition. This dignity Yahia held for some years, and when increasing infirmities obliged him to resign it, the Khaliph conferred it upon his second son Jaafer.

Jaafer's abilities were formed to adorn every situation; independent of his hereditary virtues, he was the most admired writer and the most eloquent speaker of his age; and during the time he was in office, he displayed at once the accuracy of a man of business and the comprehensive ideas of a statesman.

But the brilliancy of Jaafer's talents rendered him more acceptable to his master in the capacity of a companion than in that of a minister. Haroun resolved therefore, that state affairs should no longer deprive him of the pleasure he derived from Jaafer's society, and accordingly made him relinquish his post, and appointed his brother Fadhel, a man of severer manners, grand vizir in his room.

For seventeen years the two brothers were all-powerful in Bagdad and throughout the empire, but as often happens in the East, their authority was overturned in a moment, and their whole house involved in ruin.

The disgrace and consequent ill-treatment of the Barmecides throw an eternal stain upon the memory of Alrashid; and the causes to which they are commonly attributed seem so vague and romantic, that we can scarce imagine a prince like Haroun could ever have been actuated by such motives to commit such enormities.

The reason for their disgrace most generally received is as follows.

The Khaliph had a sister called Abassa, of whom he was passionately fond, and whose company he preferred to every thing but the conversation of Jaafer.

These two pleasures he would fain have joined together, by carrying Jaafer with him in his visits to Abassa, but the laws of the Huram, which forbad any one except a near relation being introduced there, made that impossible, and he was obliged to be absent either from his sister or from his favourite. At length he discovered a method which he hoped would enable him to enjoy at the same time the society of these two persons, who were so dear to him. This was to unite Jaafer and Abassa in marriage. They were married accordingly; but with this express condition, that they should never meet, except in the presence of the Khaliph.

Their interviews however were very frequent, and as neither could be insensible of the amiable qualities which the other possessed, a mutual affection took place between them. Blinded by their passion, they forgot the Khaliph's injunction, and the consequences of their intercourse were but too apparent. Abassa was delivered of a son, whom they privately sent to be educated at Mecca.

*For some time their amour was concealed from Alrashid: but the Khaliph having at length received intelligence of it, he gave way to his rage and determined to take the most severe revenge. In consequence of this cruel resolve, he immediately commanded Jaafer to be put to death, and the whole race of Barmec to be deprived of their possessions and thrown into prison. These orders were obeyed; Jaafer was beheaded in the antechamber of the royal apartment, whither he had come to request an interview with the implacable Haroun, and his father and brothers perished in confinement.*

*Some of the consolatory words which* Yahia *delivered to his unfortunate family, whilst they were in prison, are preserved by* Ben Shonah: *" Power and wealth," said the venerable old man, " were but a loan with which fortune entrusted us; we ought to be thankful that we have enjoyed these blessings so long, and we ought to console ourselves for their loss, by the reflection that our fate will afford a perpetual example to others of their instability."*

The fall of the house of Barmec was considered as a general calamity; by their courtesy, their abilities and their virtues, they had endeared themselves to every one; and, according to an oriental writer, they enjoyed the singular felicity of being loved as much when in the plentitude of their power, as in a private station; and of being praised as much after their disgrace and ruin, as when they were at the summit of their prosperity.

---

No, Barmec! time hath never shewn
   So sad a change of wayward fate;
Nor sorrowing mortals ever known
   A grief so true, a loss so great.

Spouse of the world! Thy soothing breast
   Did balm to every woe afford;
And now no more by thee caress'd,
   The widow'd world bewails her Lord.

## XVI.

### AN
# EPIGRAM,
### UPON
## TAHER BEN HOSEIN,
#### WHO WAS AMBIDEXTER, AND ONE EYED.

*TAHER BEN HOSEIN appears to have been the most celebrated general of his time.* He commanded the forces of *Mamun*, second son to *Haroun Alrashid*, and it was chiefly owing to his abilities that *Mamun* arrived at the throne.

Haroun had left the principal part of his dominions, along with the title of Khaliph, to his eldest son *Amin*; the province of Khorassan was all he bestowed upon *Mamun*, and even of this, *Amin* resolved to deprive his brother.

When he had formed his plan, he sent for *Mamun* to Bagdad, in order to make him give an account of his administration: but *Mamun*, aware of the Khaliph's designs, refused to obey; and upon this refusal war was openly declared between the two brothers.

The contest however was not long, for Taher Ben Hosein being appointed Mamun's general, he made an unexpected attack upon Amin's forces, and after compleatly routing them, marched to Bagdad, and took possession of the city in the name of his master.

Amin was engaged in a game at chess when his capital surrendered, but instead of being affected with this event, he requested the person who brought the intelligence, not to interrupt him, as he was upon the point of giving his adversary check mate. Such an opponent could not be very formidable to Taher; he pursued his advantages, and in a short time became master of the imperial palace and of the person of Amin. This weak prince soon after suffered death by Taher's command, and Mamun was proclaimed Khaliph in his stead.

Mamun evinced his gratitude to his general by appointing him hereditary lord of Khorassan; a dignity which Taher's posterity enjoyed for many years.

This is the first example of the dismemberment of the Arabian empire; an example however so frequently followed by Mamun's successors, that at length little was left to the Khaliphs except a few empty titles and a precarious authority within the walls of Bagdad.

This epigram upon Taher reminds us of the following well-known lines, upon a brother and sister, both extremely beautiful, but who had each lost an eye; and it is curious to observe how easily the same idea is modified by a different poet into a satire or a panegyric:

*Lumine dextro Acon, capta est Leonilla sinistro,*
  *Sed potis est formâ vincere uterque deos:*
*Alme puer, lumen quod habes concede sorori,*
  *Sic tu cæcus Amor, sic erit illa Venus.*

*An eye both Lycidas and Julia want,*
  *Yet each is fairer than the Gods above;*
*Could'st thou, sweet youth, thine eye to Julia grant,*
  *Thou would'st be Cupid, she the Queen of love.*

---

A PAIR of right hands and a single dim eye
Must form not a man, but a monster, they cry:
Change a hand to an eye, good Taher, if you can,
And a monster perhaps may be chang'd to a man.

## XVII.

### THE
# ADIEU,
### BY
## ABOU MOHAMMED.

*THIS beautiful little composition was sung by Abou Mohammed, a musician of Bagdad, before the Khaliph Wathek, as a specimen of his musical talents; and such were its effects upon the Khaliph, that he immediately testified his approbation of the performance by throwing his own robe over the shoulders of Abou Mohammed, and ordering him a present of an hundred thousand dirhems.*

*Wathek was the ninth Khaliph of the house of Abbas, and son to Motassem, the youngest of Haroun Alrashid's children.*

*He succeeded his father A. H. 227; and died after a short reign of five years.*

*Wathek was not deficient either in virtue or abilities. He not only admired and countenanced literature and the sciences, but in several branches of them, particularly poetry and music, was himself a proficient: he was brave, liberal and just. But notwithstanding his good qualities, he could never render himself popular with his subjects, on account of his being unfortunately attached to the heterodox opinion that the Koran had been created. In consequence of this prejudice against him, his reign was perpetually disturbed by riots and insurrections; in one of which he had nearly been deposed, and Ahmed Ben Nassar, a Doctor of Bagdad, the most strenuous supporter of the Koran's eternity, elected Khaliph in his room.*

*Nor was this dislike confined only to those of his own time; many succeeding historians have adopted the same ideas, and represented Wathek as a monster of folly and impiety. But we cannot easily give credit to these assertions, with respect to a prince who encouraged industry with so much judgement, that not a beggar could be seen throughout his empire, and who died with the following pious ejaculation in his mouth: " King of heaven! whose dominion is everlasting; have mercy on a wretched prince whose reign is transitory."*

The boatmen shout, " 'Tis time to part,
  No longer we can stay;"—
'Twas then MAIMUNA taught my heart
  How much a glance could say.

With trembling steps to me she came;
  "Farewell," she would have cried,
But ere her lips the word could frame
  In half-form'd sounds it died.

Then bending down, with looks of love,
  Her arms she round me flung,
And, as the gale hangs on the grove,
  Upon my breast she hung.

My willing arms embrac'd the maid,
  My heart with raptures beat;
While she but wept the more and said,
  "Would we had never met!"

## XVIII.

### ABOU TEMAN HABIB
### TO HIS MISTRESS,
#### WHO HAD FOUND FAULT WITH HIM FOR PROFUSION.

*ABOU TEMAN is reckoned the most excellent of all the Arabian poets; and I regret that I have not been able to give a more adequate specimen of his talents.*

*He was born near Damascus A. H.* 190, *and educated in Egypt; but the principal part of his life was spent at Bagdad, under the patronage of the Abbasside Khaliphs.*

*The presents he is reported to have received from these princes, and the respect with which he was treated by them, are so extravagant, that one can scarce give credit to the accounts of historians. For a single poem, which he presented to one of them, he was rewarded with fifty thousand pieces of gold, and at the same time assured, that this pecuniary favour was infinitely below the obligation he had conferred: and upon reciting an Elegy he had composed* on the death of some great man, he was told, that no one could be said to die who had been celebrated by Abou Temun.

This poet expired at Mousel, before he had quite reached his fortieth year. His early death had been already predicted by a contemporary writer, in these words: " The mind of Abou Temun must soon wear out his body, as the blade of an Indian scymeter destroys its scabbard."

Abou Temun was the compiler of the Ilamasa, a miscellany to which this compilation has been not a little indebted.

---

UNGENEROUS and mistaken maid,
    To scorn me thus because I'm poor!
Canst thou a liberal hand upbraid
    For dealing round some worthless ore?


To spare's the wish of little souls,
    The great but gather to bestow;
Yon current down the mountain rolls,
    And stagnates in the swamp below.

## XIX.

### TO A
# FEMALE CUPBEARER,
### BY
## ABD ALSALAM BEN RAGBAN.

*ABD ALSALAM was a poet more remarkable for abilities than morality.*

*We may form an idea of the nature of his compositions from the nickname he acquired amongst his contemporaries of* ديك الجن *i. e. Cock of the evil Genii. He died in the 236ᵈ. year of the Hejra, aged near eighty.*

C OME, L EILA, fill the goblet up,
    Reach round the rosy wine,
Think not that we will take the cup
    From any hand but thine.

A draught like this 'twere vain to seek,
    No grape can such supply;
It steals its tint from L<small>EILA</small>'s cheek,
    Its brightness from her eye.

## XX.

## SONGS,

BY

### MASHDUD, RAKEEK AND RAIS,

THE THREE MOST CELEBRTED IMPROVISATORI POETS IN BAGDAD, AT AN ENTERTAINMENT GIVEN BY ABOU ISY, SON OF THE KHALIPH MOTAWAKKEL.

---

*THE preface with which these poems are accompanied in the Mostatraf, at the same time that it explains the cause of their composition, gives no bad picture of Arabian manners during the flourishing period of the Khaliphat.*

"*I was one day going to the Mosque,*" "*says Abou Akramah, an author who supported himself at Bagdad by the profits of his pen,*" *in order to see if I could pick up any little anecdote which might serve for the groundwork of a tale. As I passed the gate of Abou Isy, son to the Khaliph Motawakkel, I saw Mashdud, the celebrated extempore poet, standing near it.*

"Mashdud saluted me, and asked whither I was going; I answered, to the Mosque, and confessed without reserve the business which drew me thither. The poet, upon hearing this, pressed me to accompany him to the palace of Abou Isy: I declined however complying with his solicitations, conscious of the impropriety of intruding myself uninvited into the presence of a person of such rank and consequence. But Abou Isy's porter, overhearing our conversation, declared that he would put an end to my difficulties in a moment, by acquainting his master with my arrival.

"He did so; and in a short time two servants appeared, who took me up in their arms, and carried me into a most magnificent apartment, where their master was sitting. Upon my introduction, I could not help feeling a little confused, but the prince soon made me easy, by calling out in a good natured manner; "Why do you stand blushing there, you simpleton? Take a seat." I obeyed; and in a few minutes a sumptuous collation was brought in, of which I partook. Nor was the juice of the grape forgotten: a cupbearer, brilliant as the morning star, poured out wine for us more sparkling than the beams of the sun reflected by a mirror.

"After the entertainment I arose, and having invoked every blessing to be showered down upon the head of my bounteous host, *I was preparing to withdraw. But Abou Isy prevented me, and immediately ordered Mashdud, together with Rakeek and Rais, two musicians, whose fame was almost equal to Mashdud's, to be called in. They appeared accordingly; and having taken their places, Mashdud gave us the following satyric song:*

MASHDUD ON THE MONKS OF KHABBET.

TENANTS of yon hallow'd fane!
  Let me your devotions share,
There unceasing raptures reign —
  None are ever sober there.

Crowded gardens, festive bowers
  Ne'er shall claim a thought of mine;
You can give in KHABBET's towers —
  Purer joys and brighter wine.

Tho' your pallid faces prove
  How you nightly vigils keep,
'Tis but that you ever love
  Flowing goblets more than sleep.

Tho' your eye balls dim and sunk
  Stream in penitential guise,
'Tis but that the wine you've drunk
  Bubbles over from your eyes.

---

*He had no sooner finished, than Rakeek began, and in the same versification, and to the same air, sung as follows:*

---

RAKEEK TO HIS FEMALE COMPANIONS.

Tho' the peevish tongues upbraid,
  Tho' the brows of wisdom scowl,
Fair ones here on roses laid,
  Careless will we quaff the bowl.

Let the cup, with nectar crown'd,
  Thro' the grove its beams display,
It can shed a lustre round,
  Brighter than the torch of day.

Let it pass from hand to hand,
  Circling still with ceaseless flight,
Till the streaks of gray expand
  O'er the fleeting robe of night.

As night flits, she does but cry,
  " Seize the moments that remain"—
Thus our joys with yours shall vie,
  Tenants of yon hallow'd fane!

*It was Rais's turn next, who charmed us with this plaintive little dialogue supposed to pass betwixt himself and a lady:*

### DIALOGUE BY RAIS.

#### RAIS.

MAID of sorrow, tell us why
   Sad and drooping hangs thy head?
Is it grief that bids thee sigh?
   Is it sleep that flies thy bed?

#### LADY.

Ah! I mourn no fancied wound,
   Pangs too true this heart have wrung,
Since the snakes which curl around
   SELIM's brows my bosom stung.

Destin'd now to keener woes,
   I must see the youth depart;
He must go, and as he goes
   Rend at once my bursting heart.

Slumber may desert my bed,
   'Tis not slumber's charms I seek —
'Tis the robe of beauty spread
   O'er my SELIM's rosy cheek.

## XXI.

### TO A
# LADY WEEPING,
### BY
## EBN ALRUMI.

*EBN ALRUMI is reckoned by the Arabian writers as one of the most excellent of all their poets. He was by birth a Syrian, and passed the greatest part of his time at Emessa, where he died A. H. 283.*

*Alrumi attempted every species of poetry, and he attempted none in which he did not succeed. But he requires no further encomium when we say, that he was the favourite author of the celebrated Avicenna, who employed a great part of his leizure hours in writing a commentary upon the works of Ebn Alrumi.*

When I beheld thy blue eye shine
　Thro' the bright drop that pity drew,
I saw beneath those tears of thine
　A blue-eyed violet bath'd in dew.


The violet ever scents the gale,
　Its hues adorn the fairest wreath,
But sweetest thro' a dewy veil
　Its colours glow, its odors breathe.


And thus thy charms in brightness rise—
　When wit and pleasure round thee play,
When mirth sits smiling in thine eyes,
　Who but *admires* their sprightly ray?
But when thro' pity's flood they gleam,
Who but must *love* their soften'd beam?

## XXII.
### ON A
## VALETUDINARIAN,
#### BY THE SAME.

So careful is Isa and anxious to last,
    So afraid of himself is he grown,
He swears thro' two nostrils the breath goes too fast,
    And he's trying to breathe thro' but one.

## XXIII.
### ON A
## MISER,
#### BY THE SAME.

"Hang her, a thoughtless, wasteful fool,
    She scatter's corn where'er she goes"—
Quoth Hassan, angry at his mule,
    That dropt a dinner to the crows.

# XXIV.

TO

## CASSIM OBID ALLAH,
### THE VIZIR OF MOTADHED, UPON THE DEATH OF ONE OF HIS SONS,

BY

### ALY BEN AHMED BEN MANSOUR.

*ALY BEN AHMED* distinguished himself in prose as well as poetry, and an historical work, of considerable reputation, of which he was the author, is still extant. But he principally excelled in satire, and so fond was he of indulging this dangerous talent, that no one escaped his lash; if he could only bring out a sarcasm, it was matter of indifference to him whether an enemy or a brother smarted under its severity. He died at Bagdad A. H. 302.

The person to whom this epigram is addressed, Cassim Obid Allah, was successively vizir to Motadhed and

Moctafi his son, the sixteenth and seventeenth Khaliphs of the house of Abbas; the latter of whom was principally indebted to the activity of Obid Allah for his exaltation to the throne.

This vizir died A. H. 294, having been intrusted with the chief direction of affairs at Bagdad for near fifteen years.

The office of vizir seems to have been almost hereditary in the family of Obid Allah; his son Hosein filled that post under Moctader, the successor of Moctofi, and his son Mohammed under Kaher, who succeeded to Moctader. With them ended the authority of the grand vizirs; for after the death of Kaher, the Khaliph Radhi created a new officer, to whom he gave the title of Emir Alomra, i. e. Commander of the Commanders, whom he invested with all the substantial power of the state.

It is not easy to say which of the above mentioned sons of Obid Allah is the one pointed at in these verses of Ben Ahmed: if we judge from their characters, the sarcasm might apply to either without much impropriety; for Hosein was condemned to suffer punishment for his impiety, in the reign of Radhi, and Mohammed was the favourite minister of Kaher, who appears to have been the greatest monster that ever presided over the Khaliphat.

Poor Cassim! thou art doom'd to mourn
    By destiny's decree;
Whatever happen it must turn
    To misery for thee.

Two sons hadst thou, the one thy pride,
    The other was thy pest;
Ah, why did cruel death decide
    To snatch away the best?

No wonder thou should'st droop with woe,
    Of such a child bereft;
But now thy tears must doubly flow,
    For ah!—the other's left.

## XXV.
### TO
# A FRIEND,
#### UPON HIS
## BIRTH DAY.

*THE thought, contained in these lines, appears so natural and so obvious, that one wonders it did not occur to all who have attempted to write upon a birth day or a death. To me however it was perfectly novel.*

*The Persian verses, given in the Asiatic Miscellany, Vol. ii. Pag. 374. seem to be a translation from our Arabian author.*

WHEN born, in tears we saw thee drown'd,
While thine assembled friends around,
   With smiles their joy confest;
So live, that at thy parting hour,
They may the flood of sorrow pour,
   And thou in smiles be drest!

# XXVI.

## ON A CAT THAT WAS KILLED AS SHE WAS ATTEMPTING TO ROB A DOVE-HOUSE.

### BY

## IBN ALALAF ALNAHARWANY.

*THE occasion of this odd composition and its real intent are variously related.*

*Some say that it means no more than it pretends to do, and that it was actually composed upon the death of a favourite cat.*

*Others tell us that the poet here laments the misfortunes of Abdallah Ebn Motaz, who was raised to the Khaliphat by a popular tumult in the year of the Hejra 296, and, after enjoying his dignity a single day, put to death by his rival Moctader. As Abou Becr durst not shew his grief for Abdallah in a more open manner he invented, according to these authors, the following allegory, in which the fate of Abdallah is represented under that of a cat.*

But the opinion most generally received is that Abou Becr composed these verses as an Elegy upon the death of a private friend whose name is not known, but who, like Abdallah, owed his ruin to the rash gratification of a headstrong passion.

This young man entertained an affection for a favourite female slave belonging to the vizir Ali Ben Isa, and was equally beloved by her in return. Their amour had been concealed for some time, but the lovers being one day unfortunately surprized in each other's company by the jealous vizir, he sacrificed them both to his fury, upon the spot.

The author of this production was a native of Naharwan, but he lived principally at Bagdad, where he expired A. H. 318, at the advanced age of an hundred.

He is represented to have had a most voracious appetite, and as little delicacy in the choice of his food. Of this Nuvari relates the following ludicrous instance.

The poet one day mounted his ass, in order to pay a visit to a nobleman in Bagdad. He was introduced into the saloon, and in the mean time the attendants conducted his ass into the kitchen, where it was killed and dressed, and at the proper time served up to Abou Becr at table. The poet relished his dinner so much, that he devoured every morsel which was set before him, declaring he had *never tasted such excellent veal in his life. When evening approached, he called for his ass, that he might return home; but the animal was no where to be found; and at length they confessed the trick which had been put upon him. The nobleman however made him a present which amply compensated for his loss, and he took leave, perfectly satisfied with his entertainment.*

---

POOR Puss is gone! 'Tis fate's decree —
   Yet I must still her loss deplore,
For dearer than a child was she,
   And ne'er shall I behold her more.

With many a sad presaging tear
   This morn I saw her steal away,
While she went on without a fear
   Except that she should miss her prey.

I saw her to the dove-house climb,
   With cautious feet and slow she stept,
Resolv'd to balance loss of time
   By eating faster than she crept.

Her subtle foes were on the watch,
   And mark'd her course, with fury fraught,
And while she hoped the birds to catch,
   An arrow's point the huntress caught.

In fancy she had got them all,
   And drunk their blood and suck'd their breath;
Alas! she only got a fall,
   And only drank the draught of death.

Why, why was pigeon's flesh so nice,
   That thoughtless cats should love it thus?
Hadst thou but liv'd on rats and mice,
   Thou hadst been living still, poor Puss.

Curst be the taste, howe'er refin'd,
   That prompts us for such joys to wish,
And curst the dainty where we find
   Destruction lurking in the dish.

## XXVIII.

AN

E P I G R A M

UPON

EBN NAPHTA-WAH,

BY

MOHAMMED BEN ZEID ALMOTAKALAM.

*MOHAMMED BEN ARFA, here called Naphta-wah, was descended from a noble family in Khorassan. He applied himself to study with indefatigable perseverance, and was a very voluminous author in several branches of literature, but he is chiefly distinguished as a grammarian. He died in the year of the Hejra* 323.

*The following verses are inserted principally to shew that the* Charade, *a species of riddle which we borrowed from the French a few years ago, has been long fashionable in the East.*

*In order to understand Ben Zeid's Charade, we must remark that, in Arabic,* Naphta *signifies a combustible not very much unlike our gunpowder, and that* Wah *is an exclamation of sorrow.*

---

BY the *former* with ruin and death we are curst,
In the *latter* we grieve for the ills of the first;
And as for the *whole*, where together they meet,
It's a drunkard, a liar, a thief and a cheat.

## XXVIII.

# F I R E,

### A

## R I D D L E.

*THIS composition seems a fit supplement to the preceding one; notwithstanding its absurdity, however, I have ventured to insert it, merely to shew that this mode of trifling was not unknown to the Orientals. It is taken from the Mostatraf, where a great number of similar productions on various subjects are preserved.*

T HE loftiest cedars I can eat,
   Yet neither paunch nor mouth have I,
I storm whene'er you give me meat,
   Whenc'er you give me drink, I die.

## XXIX.

### TO

# A LADY
## UPON SEEING HER BLUSH,
### BY
# THE KHALIPH RADHI BILLAH.

---

*RADHI BILLAH, son to Moctadher, was the twentieth Khaliph of the house of Abbas, and the last of these princes who possessed any substantial power.*

*By the thoughtlessness of Radhi's predecessors, in erecting the different provinces of their empire into independent sovereignties, the dominion of the Khaliphs had been reduced to little more than the space circumscribed by the walls of Bagdad; and by an imprudent act of his own, in abolishing the civil office of vizir, and appointing a military person to superintend the government, the authority of the Khaliphs was in fact annihilated. This officer was entitled* Emir Alomm, *i. e. Commander of the Commanders.*

Radhi Billah however, during his own life, still enjoyed the external marks of royalty; he had the usual number of guards and attendants, and his houshold establishment was upon the same footing as that of the ancient Khaliphs.

But after the decease of Radhi, which happened in the 329$^{th}$. year of the Hejra, these distinctions were withdrawn; the Commanders of the faithful saw themselves reduced to a scanty allowance, precluded from interfering with any business, except the direction of some religious ceremonies, and considered as little else than a necessary appendage to the court of the Emir Alomra.

Notwithstanding his political faults, Radhi Billah is universally represented to have been a man of talents; and the two following compositions will shew that he was not deficient in poetical merit. The latter of these is rendered peculiarly interesting from the situation of its author, who if he wanted prudence to foresee or vigour to extricate himself from his misfortunes, at least appears to have possessed sensibility to feel and genius to express them.

L̲EILA, whene'er I gaze on thee
My alter'd cheek turns pale,
While upon thine, sweet maid, I see
A deep'ning blush prevail.

Leila, shall I the cause impart
    Why such a change takes place?
The crimson stream deserts my heart,
    To mantle on thy face.

## XXX.

### ON
### THE VICISSITUDES OF LIFE,
#### BY THE SAME.

MORTAL joys, however pure,
    Soon their turbid source betray;
Mortal bliss, however sure,
    Soon must totter and decay.

Ye who now, with footsteps keen,
    Range through hopes' delusive field,
Tell us what the smiling scene
    To your ardent grasp can yield?

Other youths have oft before
   Deem'd their joys would never fade,
Till themselves were seen no more,
   Swept into oblivion's shade.

Who, with health and pleasure gay,
   E'er his fragile state could know,
Were not age and pain to say —
   Man is but the child of woe?

## XXXI.

### TO A DOVE,

#### BY SERAGE ALWARAK.

THE Dove, to ease an aching breast,
  In piteous murmurs vents her cares;
Like me she sorrows, for opprest,
  Like me, a load of grief she bears.

Her plaints are heard in every wood,
  While I would fain conceal my woes;
But vain's my wish, the briny flood,
  The more I strive, the faster flows.

Sure, gentle Bird, my drooping heart
   Divides the pangs of love with thine,
And plaintive murm'rings are *thy* part,
   And silent grief and tears are *mine*.

## XXXII.
### ON
# A THUNDER STORM,
### BY
## IBRAHIM BEN KHIRET ABOU ISAAC.

BRIGHT smil'd the morn, till o'er its head
The clouds in thicken'd foldings spread
    A robe of sable hue;
Then, gathering round day's golden king,
They stretch'd their wide o'ershadowing wing,
    And hid him from our view.

The rain his absent beams deplor'd,
And, soften'd into weeping, pour'd
    Its tears in many a flood;
The lightening laught, with horrid glare;
The thunder growl'd, in rage; the air
    In silent sorrow stood.

## XXXIII.

## SAIF ADDAULET,
### SULTAN OF ALEPPO,
### TO
### HIS FAVOURITE MISTRESS.

*SAIF ADDAULET was one of those princes who erected an independent sovereignty out of the ruins of the Khaliphat.*

*He was descended from the house of Hamadan, a family of Arabian extraction, which had established itself in Syria during the reign of the Khaliph Moctafi, where it soon rendered itself too powerful to be controuled by the feeble government of Bagdad.*

*Saif Addaulet made himself master of the city and district of Aleppo about the year of the Hejra 333, and from this time till his death, he was engaged in a perpetual warfare with the Despots of Egypt, the Emir Alomras of Bagdad, and the Greek Emperors, who adjoined to his territories on the different sides. And so successful were his* military operations, that in 356, the year of his decease, he had obtained the entire dominion of Cilicia and Armenia, together with the greatest part of Syria, and was enabled to leave an undisturbed possession of these provinces to his son.

The court of Aleppo, during Saif Addaulet's reign, was the most polished in the East; the Sultan and his brothers were all eminent for poetical talents, and whoever excelled, either in literature or science, was sure of obtaining their patronage; so that at a time when not only Europe, but great part of Asia, was sunk in the profoundest ignorance, the Sultan of Aleppo could boast of such an assemblage of genius, at his court, as few sovereigns have ever been able to bring together.

The occasion upon which the present little production of Saif Adduulet was composed, is thus related by Elmacin: the Sultan having conceived a passion for a princess of the blood royal, gave such public marks of the preference he entertained for her, that the ladies of his Harem took alarm, and resolved to rid themselves of the object of their jealousy by means of poison.

Saif Addaulet, however, obtained intelligence of their design, and determined to prevent it, by transporting the princess to a castle at some distance from Aleppo; and whilst she remained in this solitude, he addressed the following verses to her;

I SAW their jealous eyeballs roll,
   I saw them mark each glance of mine,
I saw thy terrors, and my soul
   Shar'd ev'ry pang that tortur'd thine.

In vain, to wean my constant heart,
   Or quench my glowing flame, they strove;
Each deep-laid scheme, each envious art,
   But wak'd my fears for her I love.

'Twas this compell'd the stern decree,
   That forc'd thee to those distant towers,
And left me nought but love for thee,
   To cheer my solitary hours.

Yet let not ABLA sink deprest,
   Nor separation's pangs deplore;
We meet not—'tis to meet more blest;
   We parted—'tis to part no more.

## XXXIV.

### ON THE CRUCIFIXION OF EBN BAKIAH, BY ABOU HASSAN ALANBARY.

*EBN BAKIAH* was vizir to *Azzad Addaulet* or *Bachteir*, Emir Alomra of Bagdad, under the Khaliphs, *Moti Lillah* and *Tay Lillah*; but *Azzad Addaulet* being deprived of his office, and driven from Bagdad by *Adhed Addaulet*, Sultan of Persia, Ebn Bakiah was seized upon and crucified at the gates of the city, by order of the conqueror.

The mode of punishment inflicted on the vizir gave occasion to the following quibbling composition, which appears to an European more remarkable for its unfeelingness than for its ingenuity: amongst the Orientals however, who prefer this kind of jeu de mots to every other species of wit, it has always been so much admired, that there is scarce any historian of those times who has not inserted in his work a copy of the verses upon Ebn Bakiah.

Azzad Addaulet and Adhed Addaulet were both descended from the house of Bowiah, a house which, from the meanest original, raised itself to the sovereignty of great part of Asia.

Bowiah, a poor fisherman in the province of Dilam, had three sons, who began the world by officiating as servants in the camp of a petty Persian despot. But, in a short time, they distinguished themselves so highly for talents and valour, that their services were courted by the greatest princes; they were placed at the head of armies, had the direction of cabinets, and saw themselves honoured and caressed wherever they appeared. The ambition of the Bowiahdes kept pace with their rising fortune, and they soon aimed at sovereign power; nor were their wishes long ungratified, for after a few years, the eldest obtained the crown of Persia, and the youngest was appointed Emir Alomra to the Khaliphs.

Azzad Addaulet was son of the Emir Alomra, and after the death of his father administered the government of Bagdad; Adhed Addaulet, son to the second brother, succeeded his uncle in the kingdom of Persia.

For some time the two cousins kept up an intercourse of friendship, but the Sultan of Persia, conscious of his power, at length determined to unite all the possessions of the family in his own person, and having declared war against Azzad Addaulet, he brought an immense force to attack Bagdad; the Emir Alomra, unable to make any effectual resistance, fled before him, and the Persian monarch assumed the vacant dignity. By this event the city and territory of Bagdad were annexed to Adhed Addaulet's empire, which now comprehended the principal part of the Asiatic dominions of the ancient Khaliphat.

Adhed Addaulet died in the year of the Hejra 370: his descendants, the princes of the house of Bowiah, remained in possession of Persia only till the year 420; when they were expelled by Mahmoud Guzni, founder of the dynasty of Guznivides. The branch of Adhed Addaulet's family, which was settled at Bagdad, continued masters of that city and its dependencies, till the year 450; when the Seljuk Sultans of Iran wrested from them their authority, and reduced the family of Bowiah to its original insignificance.

WHATE'ER thy fate, in life and death,
  Thou'rt doom'd *above* us still to rise,
Whilst at a distance far *beneath*
  We view thee with admiring eyes.

The gazing crouds still *round* thee throng,
  Still to thy well-known voice repair,
As when erewhile thy hallow'd tongue
  Pour'd in the Mosque the solemn prayer.

Still, generous Vizir, we survey
  Thine arms *extended* o'er our head,
As lately, in the festive day,
  When they were *stretch'd* thy gifts to shed.

Earth's narrow bound'ries strove in vain
  To limit thy aspiring mind,
And now we see thy dust disdain
  Within her breast to be confin'd.

The earth's too small for one so great,
    Another mansion thou shalt have —
The clouds shall be thy winding sheet,
    The spacious vault of heaven, thy grave.

## XXXV.

### ON THE
# CAPRICES OF FORTUNE,
#### BY
## SHEMS ALMAALI CABUS,
##### THE DETHRONED SULTAN OF GEORGIA.

*HISTORY can shew few princes so amiable and few so unfortunate as Shems Almaali Cabus. He is described as possessed of almost every virtue and every accomplishment: his piety, justice, generosity and humanity, are universally celebrated; nor was he less conspicuous for intellectual powers; his genius was at once penetrating, solid and brilliant, and he distinguished himself equally as an orator, a philosopher and a poet. In such estimation were his writings held, that the most careless productions of his pen were preserved as models of composition, and we are told that a famous vizir of Persia could never open even an official dispatch from Shems Almaali without exclaiming, " This is written with the feather of a celestial bird."*

Shems Almaali ascended the throne of Georgia upon the death of his brother, A. H. 366; and during a reign of thirty-five years made the Georgians happy by his administration. His ruin was at length occasioned by an unfortunate piece of generosity.

In a contest between Mowid Addaulet and Faker Addaulet, two rival princes of the house of Bowiah, the latter had been overcome by his brother, and with difficulty escaped into Georgia, where Shems Almaali afforded him an asylum. Mowid Addaulet considered the kindness shewn to his brother as an insult to himself, and resolving upon revenge, he overran Georgia with a numerous army, and obliged Faker Addaulet and Shems Almaali to fly for refuge to the mountains of Khorassan. For three years the exiled princes led a wandering and uncomfortable life, surrounded by danger and harassed by necessity; but at the end of that period Mowid Addaulet died, and Faker Addaulet, without opposition, assumed the sceptre of Persia.

Shems Almaali, as was natural, expected to participate in his friend's good fortune, and persuaded himself that he should not only regain the kingdom of Georgia, but that every favour would be heaped upon him which it was in the power of the Persian monarch to bestow. He was disappointed; for Faker Addaulet with unparalleled ingratitude refused even to restore his hereditary dominions, and the unfortunate Shems Almaali, unable to assert his claim by arms, remained for fourteen years longer in exile. At length however Faker Addaulet died, and Shems Almaali was invited by the general voice of his subjects to return to Georgia and reassume the government. He accepted their invitation; and was no sooner settled upon the throne than he applied himself with his former assiduity to promote the welfare of his kingdom.

But the Georgians were now become unfit for such a sovereign: during his long absence, a thousand abuses had crept into every department of the state, which the great men who profited by them were unwilling to see corrected. Shems Almaali however was determined to bring about a reform, whatever might be the consequence. But the attempt was fatal to him, for a number of the principal persons of the kingdom, disgusted at his severity, at length conspired together to deprive him of the sovereignty, and, taking advantage of his son's absence, they rushed upon him unawares, and bore him off, from his tent, to a place of confinement.

After they had secured Shems Almaali, they dispatched messengers to his son Manujeher, informing him of what they had done, and offering him the throne, upon condition that he would unite with them in the deposition of his father. The young prince pretended to accede to their *proposal*, and was accordingly proclaimed sovereign of Georgia.

But *Manujeher* was no sooner in possession of the throne, than he flew to his father's prison, and prostrating himself before the old monarch, declared that he had only accepted the crown with a view of preserving it for his father, into whose hands he now restored it, and in whose defence he was ready to sacrifice his life.

*Shems Almaali* was charmed with his son's behaviour, but refused his offer, saying that he had now done with the world, and only wished to remain undisturbed in his present retreat, where he meant to dedicate his few surviving years to the service of God. *Manujeher* promised that every accommodation which his father desired should be amply furnished, and gave immediate orders for the purpose.

But the conspirators who had dethroned *Shems Almaali*, dreading his talents as much as they hated his virtues, were determined to put an end to their fears by his death. They made many attempts to persuade *Manujeher* to commit this horrid deed, but finding all their solicitations ineffectual, they resolved to undertake it themselves. The murder was not long delayed, and was accompanied with the aggravated guilt of unnecessary cruelty. For having gained possession of the castle, which *Shems Almaali* had *fixed upon for his retreat, they unroofed the chamber where he resided, deprived him of cloaths and every necessary, and left the aged monarch to perish with cold upon the pavement.*

*After the character given of Shems Almaali, it is almost superfluous to add that he was the patron of literature. His court abounded with men of genius from all parts of the East; amongst whom the celebrated Avicenna, who lived many years under his protection, deserves particularly to be mentioned.*

*The following verses appear to have been composed during Shems Almaali's exile in Khorassun.*

WHY should I blush that Fortune's frown
   Dooms me life's humble paths to tread?
To live unheeded, and unknown?
   To sink forgotten to the dead?

'Tis not the good, the wise, the brave,
   That surest shine, or highest rise;
The feather sports upon the wave,
   The pearl in ocean's cavern lies.

Each lesser star that studs the sphere
   Sparkles with undiminish'd light:
Dark and eclips'd alone appear
   The lord of day, the queen of night.

## XXXVI.

### ON
### LIFE.

———

THE sentiment contained in these lines is extremely similar to one in an old Greek epigram, preserved in the Anthologia. Our Arabian author, however, has expressed the idea with much greater elegance. The Greek epigram is as follows.

Παντις τω θανατω τηρυμιθα και τρεφομεσθα
Ως αγιλη χοιρων σφαζομενων αλογως.

Thus translated by Bergius;

Vivimus heu morti, morti quoque nascimur omnes
Ut grex porcorum qui temere intereunt.

Like Sheep, we're doom'd to travel o'er
   The fated track to all assign'd,
These follow those that went before,
   And leave the world to those behind.

As the flock seeks the pasturing shade,
   Man presses to the future day,
While death, amidst the tufted glade,
   Like the dun* robber, waits his prey.

* The wolf.

## XXXVII.

### EXTEMPORE VERSES UPON THE SULTAN CARAWASH, HIS PRINCIPAL MUSICIAN BARKAIDY, HIS VIZIR EBN FADHI, AND HIS CHAMBERLAIN ABOU JABER,

BY

### EBN ALRAMACRAM.

*THE occasion of the following composition is thus related by Abulfeda; Carawash, Sultan of Mousel, being one wintry evening engaged in a party of pleasure along with Barkaidy, Ebn Fahdi, Abou Jaber, and the improvisatore poet Ebn Alramacram, resolved to divert himself at the expence of his companions. He therefore ordered the poet to give a specimen of his talents, which at the same time should convey a satire upon the three courtiers, and a compliment to himself. Ebn Alramacram took his subject from the stormy appearance of the night, and immediately produced these verses.*

LOWERING as BARKAIDY's face
  The wintry night came in,
Cold as the music of his bass,
  And lengthen'd as his chin.

Sleep from my aching eyes had fled,
  And kept as far apart,
As sense from EBN FAHDI's head,
  Or virtue from his heart.

The dubious paths my footsteps balk'd,
  I slipp'd along the sod,
As if on JABER's faith I'd walk'd,
  Or on his truth had trod.

At length the rising king of day
  Burst on the gloomy wood,
Like CARAWASH's eye, whose ray
  Dispenses every good.

## XXXVIII.

ON THE

# DEATH OF A SON,

BY

## ALY BEN MOHAMMED ALTAHMANY.

*ALY BEN MOHAMMED was a native of that part of Arabia called Hejaz; and is celebrated not only as a poet, but as a politician. In the latter of these characters he undertook a commission, at the request of the Emir Alomra of Bagdad, the object of which was to excite an insurrection at Cairo, against the Egyptian Khaliph Taher Liazaz; but being detected in his intrigues, he was thrown into prison about the year 416, and soon after suffered death.*

T YRANT of man! Imperious Fate!
  I bow before thy dread decree,
Nor hope in this uncertain state
  To find a seat secure from thee.

Life is a dark, tumultuous stream,
  With many a care and sorrow foul,
Yet thoughtless mortals vainly deem
  That it can yield a limpid bowl.


Think not that stream will backward flow,
  Or cease its destin'd course to keep;
As soon the blazing spark shall glow
  Beneath the surface of the deep.


Believe not Fate at thy command
  Will grant a meed she never gave;
As soon the airy tower shall stand,
  That's built upon a passing wave.


Death is a sleep of threescore years,
  Death bids us wake and hail the light,
And man, with all his hopes and fears,
  Is but a phantom of the night.

## XXXIX.

### TO

### L E I L A.

*THIS production is taken from a collection of MS. tales in the hands of the translator. It is there given as a declaration of love from a young prince to his mistress; the lady's answer not appearing possessed of equal poetical merit, has not been inserted.*

L EILA, with too successful art,
   Has spread for me the cruel snare;
And now, when she has caught my heart,
   She laughs, and leaves it to despair.

Thus the poor sparrow pants for breath,
   Held captive by a playful boy,
And while it drinks the draught of death,
   The thoughtless child looks on with joy.

Ah! were its flutt'ring pinions free,
   Soon would it bid its chains adieu,
Or did the child its suff'rings see
   He'd pity and relieve them too.

## XL.

ON

### MODERATION IN OUR PLEASURES,

BY

ABOU ALCASSIM EBN TABATABA.

*TABATABA deduced his pedigree from Ali Ben Abou Taleb, and Fatima the daughter of Mohammed.*

*He was born at Ispahan, but passed the principal part of his life in Egypt, where he was appointed chief of the Sheriffs, i. e. the descendants of the Prophet, a dignity held in the highest veneration by every Mussulman. He died in the year of the Hejra 418, with the reputation of being one of the most excellent poets of his time.*

How oft does passion's grasp destroy
   The pleasure that it strives to gain?
How soon the thoughtless course of joy
   Is doom'd to terminate in pain?

When prudence would thy steps delay,
 She but restrains to make thee blest;
Whate'er from joy she lops away,
 But heightens and secures the rest.


Wouldst thou a trembling flame expand,
 That hastens in the lamp to die?
With careful touch, with sparing hand,
 The feeding stream of life supply.


But if thy flask profusely sheds
 A rushing torrent o'er the blaze,
Swift round the sinking flame it spreads,
 And kills the fire it fain would raise.

## XLI.

### ON

# THE VALE OF BOZAA,

### BY

### AHMED BEN YOUSEF ALMENAZY.

*BEN YOUSEF* for many years acted as vizir to *Abou Nasser,* Sultan of *Diarbeker.* His poetical talents are much praised, and he is particularly celebrated for the address he displayed while upon an embassy to the Greek emperor at *Constantinople.*

His passion for literature appears to have been extreme; the greatest part of his leisure hours were devoted to study, and such was his assiduity in collecting books, that he was able to form two very large libraries, the one at *Miaferakin* and the other at *Amid,* which for some centuries after his death were considered as the great fountains of instruction for all *Asia.*

*The following specimen of Ben Yousef's poetry must be looked upon merely as a jeu d'esprit suggested by the beauties of the vale of Bozâa, as he passed through it.*

THE intertwining boughs for thee
   Have wove, sweet dell, a verdant vest,
And thou in turn shalt give to me
   A verdant couch upon thy breast.

To shield me from day's fervid's glare
   Thine oaks their fostering arms extend,
As anxious o'er her infant care
   I've seen a watchful mother bend.

A brighter cup, a sweeter draught,
   I gather from that rill of thine,
Than maddening drunkards ever quaff'd,
   Than all the treasures of the vine.

So smooth the pebbles on its shore,
    That not a maid can thither stray,
But counts her strings of jewels o'er,
    And thinks the pearls have slipp'd away.

## XLII.

TO

## ADVERSITY,

BY

ABOU MENBAA CARAWASH,
SULTAN OF MOUSEL.

THE life of this prince was chequered with various adventures; he was perpetually engaged in contests either with the neighbouring sovereigns, or the princes of his own family.

For several years however he maintained himself in the possession of his little kingdom, notwithstanding all his enemies, and during this period rendered Mousel the seat of science and literature; but in the year of the Hejra 442, after many struggles, he was obliged to submit to his brother Abou Camel, who immediately ordered him to be seized, and conveyed to a place of security.

*While Abou Camel lived, the confinement of Carawash was made as easy as possible, he had an ample provision assigned him, and was treated with all the respect due to his former situation. But upon the demise of Abou Camel, and succession of his son Coruish, these indulgencies were taken away, and the old Sultan, unable to sustain the hardships he was now exposed to, died in prison, or, according to some authors, was murdered there by the inhuman hand of his own nephew.*

---

THOU chastening friend Adversity! 'Tis thine
The mental ore to temper and refine,
To cast in virtue's mold the yielding heart,
And honor's polish to the mind impart.

Without thy wakening touch, thy plastic aid,
I'd lain the shapeless mass that nature made;
But form'd, great artist, by thy magic hand,
I gleam a sword to conquer and command.

---

# XLIII.

## ON THE INCOMPATIBILITY OF PRIDE AND TRUE GLORY.

### BY

### ABOU ALOLA.

*ABOU ALOLA is always esteemed one of the most excellent of the Arabian poets. He was born blind, or at least lost his sight at a very early age; but this did not deter him from the pursuit of literature.*

*To prosecute his studies with more advantage, he travelled from Maara, the place of his nativity, to Bagdad, where he spent a few months in attending the lectures of the different professors at the academy of that city, and in conversing with the learned men who resorted thither from all parts of the East.*

*Abou Alóla, after this short stay in Bagdad, returned to his native cottage, which he never again quitted.*

*But notwithstanding the difficulties he laboured under from nature, and the few advantages he had received from* education, " he lived, according to Abulfeda, to know that his celebrity spread from the sequestered village which he inhabited, to the utmost confines of the globe."

Abou Alóla died at Máara in the year 449, aged 86; he attempted every species of poetry, and succeeded in all; nor was he scrupulous in the choice of his subjects, as many of his compositions seem evidently intended to turn religion into ridicule.

This disposition, together with his never eating any animal food, gave rise to a report among his contemporaries that he had abjured Mohammedanism, and become a follower of the Bramins; but several passages might be adduced from his writings, which sufficiently shew that he was as little attached to one sect of religion as to another, or rather that he was equally an enemy to all.

Abulfeda has preserved one of his epigrams, which I have endeavoured to render as follows:

Errant Islamici, servi felluntur Jesu,
   Sunt cæci Isacidæ, sunt sine corde Magi;
Dividitur mundus—pius hinc et mentis egenus
   Cernitur, atque illinc impius et sapiens.

THINK not, ABDALLAH, pride and fame
   Can ever travel hand in hand;
With breast oppos'd, and adverse aim,
   On the same narrow path they stand.

Thus youth and age together meet,
   And life's divided moments share;
This can't advance till that retreat,
   What's here increas'd, is lessen'd there.

And thus the falling shades of night
   Still struggle with the lucid ray,
And e'er they stretch their gloomy flight
   Must win the lengthen'd space from day.

# XLIV.

## UPON THE DEATH OF NEDHAM ALMOLK, VIZIR TO TOGRUL BEG, ALP ARSLAN AND MALEC SHAH, THE THREE FIRST SELJUK SULTANS OF PERSIA.

BY

## SHEBAL ADDAULET.

*SELJUK, from whom the dynasty of Seljucides or Shepherd Sultans of Persia, derived its name, came originally from Turkestan, from whence he had been driven, for a daring intrusion into the haram of his prince.*

*With a numerous tribe of friends and vassals he passed the Jaxartes, encamped near Samarcand, and embraced the religion of Mohammed. Seljuk having outlived his son, took upon him the care of his two grandsons, Togrul and Jaafer; the eldest of whom, by the general voice of his countrymen, was declared their sovereign.*

*The ambition of Togrul was equal to his valour; and he soon saw himself at the head of an extensive empire.*

By his arms the Gaznevides were expelled from the eastern provinces of Persia; in the west he annihilated the dynasty of the Bowiahdes, and obtained compleat possesion of Irak, Mousel and Bagdad. Togrul died about the year 455, and was succeeded in his kingdom and ambitious views by his nephew Alp Arslan.

The new Sultan increased the dominions of his family by the acquisition of Georgia and Armenia.

The possessions of the Greeks in Asia were now restricted to the peninsula of Anatolia, and even this province was subject to the continual depredations of the Turkish soldiers. The imperial troops fled on every side, and in one of the engagements between them and the Turks, the emperor Romancy was taken prisoner, and obliged to pay an immense ransom as the price of his liberty.

After a glorious reign of ten years, Alp Arslan fell by the hand of an assassin. He was buried in the city of Maru, and the following inscription engraved upon his tomb; O ye who have seen the glory of Alp Arslan exalted to the heavens repair to Maru, and you will behold it buried in the dust."

Malec Shah mounted the throne upon the death of his father Alp Arslan, and was not inferior to his predecessors either in talents or fortune. During his reign Syria and Turkestan were added to the Seljuk dominions, which now *extended from the Chinese frontier to the west and south, as far as the mountains of Georgia, the neighbourhood of Constantinople, the city of Jerusalem, and the confines of Arabia Felix.*

*Malec died in the year 465, and with him expired the greatness and union of the Seljuk empire.*

*While Togrul and his two successors were employed in conquests, the civil administration was committed to the vizir Nedham Almolk, who during the greatest part of the reigns of these three sovereigns governed the state with universal approbation and with almost absolute authority. His character and fate are thus described by a late elegant historian.*

"*In a period when Europe was plunged in the deepest barbarism, the light and splendor of Asia may be ascribed to the docility rather than the knowledge of the Turkish conquerors. An ample share of their wisdom and virtue is due to a Persian vizir, who ruled the empire under Alp Arslan and his son.*

"*Nedham, one of the most illustrious ministers of the East, was honoured by the Khaliph as an oracle of religion and science; he was trusted by the Sultan as the faithful vicegerent of his power and justice. After an administration of thirty years, the fame of the vizir, his wealth and even his services were transformed into crimes. He was overthrown by the insidious arts of a woman and a rival; and his fall was hastened by a rash declaration that his cap and inkhorn, the badges of his office, were connected by the divine decree with the throne and diadem of the Sultan. At the age of ninety-three years, the venerable statesman was dismissed by his master, accused by his enemies, and murdered by a fanatic. The last words of Nedham attested his innocence, and the remainder of Malec's life was short and inglorious."*

Gibbon, Vol. x.

---

THY virtues fam'd thro' every land,
    Thy spotless life, in age and death,
Prove thee a pearl\*, by nature's hand,
    Form'd out of purity and truth.


Too long its beams of orient light
    Upon a thankless world were shed;
Allah has now reveng'd the slight,
    And call'd it to its native bed.

\* Nedham, in Arabic, signifies a string of pearls.

## XLV.

**VERSES ADDRESSED BY WALADATA, DAUGHTER OF MOHAMMED ALMOSTAKFI BILLAH, KHALIPH OF SPAIN, TO SOME YOUNG MEN WHO HAD PRETENDED A PASSION FOR HERSELF AND HER COMPANIONS.**

*ALMOSTAKFI was the last Khaliph of the house of Ommiah who possessed any authority in Spain.*

*The Arabs made themselves masters of this country in the 92ᵈ. year of the Hejra; for some time it was governed by lieutenants, under the Khaliphs of Damascus; but upon the fall and extinction of the Ommiades in Asia, Abderrahman, a branch of that family, retreated into Spain, and established an independent Khaliphat at Cordova.*

*His posterity, for two hundred and eighty-five years, ruled over almost the whole peninsula, from the Pyrenees to the Atlantic; and this period is perhaps the happiest in all Spanish history; the sovereigns were wise and enlightened, the people civilized and industrious: and to such prosperity had the kingdom risen under these princes, that in the time of the third Abderrahman, the annual receipts of the royal treasury amounted to upwards of six millions stirling; a sum which in the tenth century most probably surpassed the united revenues of all the other European monarchs.*

*The power of the Khaliphs of Cordova had been for some time declining when Almostakfi ascended the throne; under this weak prince the disorders in the government increased, and upon his death the authority of the Ommiades was annihilated, and the empire split into a number of petty principalities, which were successively subjected by the arms of the Christians.*

*Casiri, to whom I am indebted for the epigram here inserted, gives the following character of the princess Waladata.*

"*Valadata Hispanici regis Mohammedis Almostakfi Billah nuncupati filia, Cordubæ nata fuit. Non pulchra minus quam ingeniosa fœmina; totam se Rhetoricæ ac Poeticæ studiis dedit. Insignium sui ævi Poetarum amicitiam colebat; frequentibus eorum colloquiis miré delectabatur; in scribendo plurimum salis habuit et acuminis, quod vel hocce disticho satis patet.*"

CASPIRI Bib. Hisp.

WHEN you told us our glances soft, timid and mild,
    Could occasion such wounds in the heart,
Can ye wonder that yours, so ungovern'd and wild,
    Some wounds to our cheeks should impart?

The wounds on our cheeks, are but transient, I own,
    With a blush they appear and decay;
But those on the heart, fickle youths, ye have shewn
    To be even more transient than they.

# XLVI.

## VERSES ADDRESSED TO HIS DAUGHTERS,

BY

### MOTAMMED BEN ABAD, SULTAN OF SEVILLE, DURING HIS IMPRISONMENT.

*SEVILLE* was one of those small sovereignties into which Spain had been divided after the extinction of the house of Ommiah.

It did not long retain its independence, and the only prince who ever presided over it as a separate kingdom seems to have been Mohammed Bed Abad, the author of these verses.

For thirty-three years he reigned over Seville and the neighbouring districts with considerable reputation, but being attacked by Joseph, son to the emperor of Morocco, at the head of a numerous army of Africans, was defeated, taken prisoner, and thrown into a dungeon, where he died in the year 488.

*The occasion of the following composition is related by Ebn Khocan, a contemporary writer, in these words:* "*Upon a certain festival, during the confinement of Motammed, he was waited upon by his children, who came to receive his blessing, and to offer up their prayers for his welfare. Amongst these, some were females, and their appearance was truly deplorable; they were naturally beauteous as the moon, but from the rags which covered them, they seemed like the moon under an eclipse; their feet were bare and bleeding, and every trace of their former splendor was compleatly effaced. At this melancholy spectacle, their unfortunate father gave way to his sorrow in the following verses:*

WITH jocund heart and chearful brow
   I us'd to hail the festal morn —
How must Motammed greet it now? —
   A prisoner helpless and forlorn.

While these dear maids in beauty's bloom,
   With want opprest, with rags o'erspread,
By sordid labors at the loom
   Must earn a poor, precarious bread.

Those feet that never touch'd the ground,
　Till musk or camphor strew'd the way,
Now bare and swoll'n with many a wound,
　Must struggle thro' the miry clay.

Those radiant cheeks are veil'd in woe,
　A shower descends from every eye,
And not a starting tear can flow,
　That wakes not an attending sigh.

Fortune that whilom own'd my sway,
　And bow'd obsequious to my nod,
Now sees me destin'd to obey,
　And bend beneath oppression's rod.

Ye mortals with success elate,
　Who bask in hope's delusive beam,
Attentive view MOTAMMED's fate,
　And own that bliss is but a dream.

## XLVII.

## A SERENADE
### TO
### HIS SLEEPING MISTRESS,
### BY
### ALY BEN ABD ALGANY OF CORDOVA.

*THIS author was by birth an African, but having passed over to Spain, he was much patronised by Motammed, Sultan of Seville.*

*After the fall of his master, Ben Abd returned into Africa, and died at Tangier A. H. 488.*

*Ben Abd wrote at a time when Arabic literature was upon the decline in Spain, and his verses are not very unlike the compositions of our own metaphysical poets in the last century.*

Sure Harut's[*] potent spells were breath'd
  Upon that magic sword, thine eye;
For if it wounds us thus while sheath'd,
  When drawn, 'tis vain its edge to fly.

How canst thou doom me, cruel fair,
  Plung'd in the hell[†] of scorn, to groan?
No idol e'er this heart could share,
  This heart has worshipp'd thee alone.

[*] A wicked angel who is permitted to tempt mankind by teaching them magic; see the legend respecting him in Sale's Koran, page 19.

[†] The poet here alludes to the punishments denounced in the Koran against those who worship a plurality of Gods: "their couch shall be in hell, and over them shall be coverings of fire." Sur. s.

## XLVIII.

### THE INCONSISTENT.

#### TO A LADY, UPON HER REFUSAL OF A PRESENT OF MELONS, AND HER REJECTION OF THE ADDRESSES OF AN ADMIRER.

WHEN I sent you my Melons, you cried out with scorn,
"They ought to be *heavy* and *wrinkled* and *yellow:*"
When I offer'd myself, whom those graces adorn,
You flouted, and call'd me an *ugly*, *old* fellow.

## XLIX.

### ON THE
# CAPTURE OF JERUSALEM
### IN THE FIRST CRUSADE,
### BY
## ALMODHAFER ALABIWERDY.

---

THE capture of *Jerusalem* took place in the 492ᵈ. year of the *Hejra*, A. D. 1099. This event is too well known to render it necessary to be dwelt upon.

For many ages the wars of the crusades were the favourite topics of history, amongst the Latins, the Greeks and the Orientals; and consequently they are described with more precision than any other transactions at the same distance of time. Of these writers, the last are undoubtedly entitled to the greatest degree of credit, both on account of their advantages with respect to local knowledge, and their superiority in general erudition.

The world has already been made acquainted with some of the Eastern Historians, many more however remain unpublished, even in our own libraries at Oxford and Cambridge, which would, no doubt, still further elucidate the occurrences of that active and tumultuous period.

In looking over these authors, I have often thought, that from the information they contain, added to what is already in our possession, an account of the Crusades might be compiled, which would not be unacceptable to the public.

Such a work, if properly executed, must throw considerable light upon the history of manners, and the progress of arts and civilization, during the middle ages; and could not but be interesting, if it tended to develope more fully a subject, which for so many centuries engaged the principal attention of mankind, from the borders of China to the Atlantic ocean; and of which the consequences are still discernible in almost every nation upon the globe.

Abiwerdy, who composed these verses, was a native of Khorassan; he died A. H. 507.

---

FROM our distended eyeballs flow
   Mingled streams of tears and blood;
No care we feel, nor wish we know,
   But who shall pour the largest flood.

But what defence can tears afford?
   What aid supply in this dread hour?
When kindled by the sparkling sword
   War's raging flames the land devour.

No more let sleep's seductive charms
   Upon your torpid souls be shed;
A crash like this, such dire alarms,
   Might burst the slumbers of the dead.

Think where your dear companions lie —
   Survey their fate, and hear their woes —
How some thro' trackless deserts fly,
   Some in the Vulture's maw repose;

While some more wretched still, must bear
   The tauntings of a Christian's tongue —
Hear this — and blush ye not to wear
   The silken robe of peace so long?

Remember what ensanguin'd showers
    The Syrian plains with crimson dyed,
And think how many blooming flowers
    In Syrian forts their beauties hide.

Arabian youths! In such a cause
    Can ye the voice of glory slight?
Warriors of Persia! Can ye pause,
    Or fear to mingle in the fight?

If neither piety nor shame
    Your breasts can warm, your souls can move,
Let emulation's bursting flame
    Wake you to vengeance and to love.

## L.

TO

# A LADY,

WHO ACCUSED HER LOVER OF FLATTERY.

No, ABLA, no — when SELIM tells
Of many an unknown grace that dwells
    In ABLA's face and mien,
When he describes the sense refin'd,
That lights thine eye, and fills thy mind,
    By thee alone unseen;

'Tis not that drunk with love he sees
Ideal charms which only please
    Thro' passion's partial veil,
'Tis not that flattery's glozing tongue
Hath basely fram'd an idle song,
    But truth that breath'd the tale.

Thine eyes unaided ne'er could trace
Each opening charm, each varied grace,
    That round thy person plays;
Some must remain conceal'd from thee,
For SELIM's watchful eye to see,
    For SELIM's tongue to praise.

One polish'd mirror can declare
That eye so bright, that face so fair,
    That cheek which shames the rose;
But how thy mantle waves behind,
How float thy tresses on the wind,
    Another only shews.

## LI.

## AN EPIGRAM

UPON

ABOU ALCHAIR SELAMU, AN EGYPTIAN PHYSICIAN,

BY

GEORGE, A PHYSICIAN OF ANTIOCH.

Whoever has recourse to thee
   Can hope for health no more,
He's launch'd into perdition's sea,
   A sea without a shore.

Where'er admission thou canst gain,
   Where'er thy phyz can pierce,
At once the Doctor they retain,
   The mourners and the hearse.

## LII.
### ON A LITTLE MAN WITH A VERY LARGE BEARD,
#### BY
#### ISAAC BEN KHALIF.

How can thy chin that burden bear?
   Is it all gravity to shock?
Is it to make the people stare?
   And be thyself a laughing stock?

When I beheld thy little feet
   After thy beard obsequious run,
I always fancy that I meet
   Some father followed by his son.

A man like thee scarce e'er appear'd —
   A beard like thine — where shall we find it?
Surely thou cherishest thy beard
   In hopes to hide thyself behind it.

## LIII.

## LAMIAT ALAJEM,

### A POEM,

BY

MAUID EDDIN ALHASSAN ABOU ISMAEL ALTOGRAI.

*ABOU ISMAEL was a native of Ispahan. He devoted himself to the service of the Seljuk Sultans of Persia, and enjoyed the confidence of Malec Shah, and his son and grandson Mohammed and Massoud, by the last of whom he was raised to the dignity of vizir.*

*Massoud however was not long in a condition to afford Abou Ismael any protection, for being attacked by his brother Mahmoud, he was defeated, and driven from Mousel, and upon the fall of his master, the vizir was seized, and thrown into prison, and at length in the year 515 sentenced to be put to death.*

( 150 )

This poem seems to have been composed in the interval of time between the flight of Massoud and the imprisonment of Abou Ismael; at least it breathes such sentiments as we might expect to proceed from a man in a similar situation.

The scene lies in the desert, where the poet is supposed to be travelling along with a caravan. The time is midnight, and while he is kept awake by his sorrows, his fellow-travellers are slumbering around him.

The author opens the poem with a panegyric upon his own integrity, and the magnanimity he has shewn under various misfortunes; these he is proceeding to recount, when he seems suddenly struck with the sight of a friend lying asleep at some distance from him — The poet adjures this friend to arise, and accompany him in an enterprize, the object of which was to visit a lady, whose habitation was in the neighbourhood — Fired with the idea of his mistress, he breaks forth into a description of the happiness of those who are admitted to her society, and resolves that nothing shall divert him from his purpose — His friend however appearing unmoved by his solicitations, he at length gives up his intention in despair, and after many bitter invectives against cowardice and sloth, returns to the subject of his misfortunes, and concludes the poem with an ardent exhortation to mistrust mankind, and in every *contingence to rely solely upon our own prudence and fortitude.*

*Such is the analysis of the Lamiat Alajem, a composition which has obtained more general approbation than almost any poem extant in the East; it is celebrated by the historians, commented upon by the critics, and quoted by the people; I have therefore given it entire from the edition of Dr. Pococke.*

*The extreme popularity of this production is a striking proof of the decay of all true taste amongst the Orientals: it were otherwise impossible that they could prefer the laboured conceits and tinsel ornaments of Abou Ismael to the simplicity of the bards of Yemun, and the elegance of the poets of Bagdad.*

---

No kind supporting hand I meet,
But Fortitude shall stay my feet;
No borrow'd splendors round me shine,
But Virtue's lustre all is mine;
A Fame unsullied still I boast,
Obscur'd, conceal'd, but never lost—
The same bright orb that led the day
Pours from the west his mellow'd ray.

ZAURA, farewell! No more I see
Within thy walls, a home for me;
Deserted, spurn'd, aside I'm toss'd,
As an old sword whose scabbard's lost:
Around thy walls I seek in vain
Some bosom that will soothe my pain—
No friend is near to breathe relief,
Or brother to partake my grief.

For many a melancholy day
Thro' desert vales I've wound my way;
The faithful beast, whose back I press,
In groans laments her lord's distress;
In every quiv'ring of my spear
A sympathetic sigh I hear;
The camel bending with his load,
And struggling thro' the thorny road,
Midst the fatigues that bear him down,
In HASSAN's woes forgets his own;

Yet cruel friends my wand'rings chide,
My sufferings slight, my toils deride.

But wealth, I own, engross'd each thought,
There was a moment when I sought
The glitt'ring stores Ambition claims
To feed the wants his fancy frames;
But now 'tis past — the changing day
Has snatch'd my high-built hopes away,
And bade this wish my labours close,
Give me not riches, but repose.

'Tis he — that mien my friend declares,
That stature, like the lance he bears;
I see that breast which ne'er contain'd
A thought by fear or folly stain'd,
Whose powers can every change obey,
In business grave, in trifles gay,

And, form'd each varying taste to please,
Can mingle dignity with ease.

What, tho', with magic influence, sleep,
O'er every closing eyelid creep:
Tho' drunk with its oblivious wine
Our comrades on their bales recline,
My Selim's trance I sure can break —
Selim, 'tis I, 'tis I who speak.
Dangers on every side impend,
And sleep'st thou, careless of thy friend?
Thou sleep'st while every star from high
Beholds me with a wakeful eye,
Thou changest, ere the changeful night
Hath streak'd her fleeting robe with white.

'Tis love that hurries me along —
I'm deaf to fear's repressive tongue —

The rocks of IDHAM I'll ascend,
Tho' adverse darts each path defend,
And hostile sabres glitter there,
To guard the tresses of the fair.

Come, SELIM, let us pierce the grove,
While night befriends, to seek my love.
The clouds of fragrance as they rise
Shall mark the place where ABLA lies.
Around her tent my jealous foes,
Like lions, spread their watchful rows;
Amidst their bands, her bow'r appears
Embosom'd in a wood of spears,
A wood still nourish'd by the dews,
Which smiles, and softest looks diffuse.

Thrice happy youths! who midst yon shades
Sweet converse hold with IDHAM's maids,

What bliss, to view them gild the hours,
And brighten wit and fancy's powers,
While every foible they disclose
New transport gives, new graces shews.
'Tis *theirs* to raise with conscious art
The *flames* of love in every heart;
'Tis *yours* to raise with festive glee
The *flames* of hospitality:
Smit by *their* glances *lovers* lie,
And helpless sink, and hopeless *die*;
While slain by you the stately steed
To crown the feast is doom'd to bleed,
To crown the feast, where copious flows
The sparkling juice that sooths your woes,
That lulls each care and heals each wound,
As the enliv'ning bowl goes round.

Amidst those vales my eager feet
Shall trace my ABLA's dear retreat,

A gale of health may hover there,
To breathe some solace to my care.
I fear not love — I bless the dart
Sent in a glance to pierce the heart:
With willing breast the sword I hail
That wounds me thro' an half-clos'd veil:
Tho' lions howling round the shade,
My footsteps haunt, my walks invade,
No fears shall drive me from the grove,
If ABLA listen to my love.
Ah, SELIM! shall the spells of ease
Thy friendship chain, thine ardor freeze!
Wilt thou exhausted thus, decline
Each gen'rous thought, each bold design?
Then far from men some cell prepare,
Or build a mansion in the air —
But yield to those, ambition's tide,
Who fearless on its waves can ride;

Enough for thee if thou receive
The scatter'd spray the billows leave.

   Contempt and want the wretch await
Who slumbers in an abject state —
Midst rushing crouds, by toil and pain
The meed of Honour we must gain;
At Honour's call, the camel hastes
Thro' trackless wilds and dreary wastes,
Till in the glorious race she find
The fleetest coursers left behind:
By toils like these alone, he cries,
Th' advent'rous youths to greatness rise;
If bloated indolence were fame,
And pompous ease our noblest aim,
The orb that regulates the day
Would ne'er from ARIES' mansion stray.

I've bent at Fortune's shrine too long—
Too oft she heard my suppliant tongue—
Too oft has mock'd my idle prayers,
While fools and knaves engross'd her cares,
Awake for them, asleep to me,
Heedless of worth she scorn'd each plea.
Ah! had her eyes, more just, survey'd
The diff'rent claims which each display'd,
Those eyes from partial fondness free
Had slept to them, and wak'd for me.

But midst my sorrows and my toils
Hope ever sooth'd my breast with smiles;
Her hand remov'd each gathering ill,
And op'd life's closing prospects still.
Yet spite of all her friendly art
The specious scene ne'er gain'd my heart;
I lov'd it not altho' the day
Met my approach, and cheer'd my way;

I loath it now the hours retreat,
And fly me with reverted feet.

  My soul from every tarnish free
May boldly vaunt her purity,
However keen, however bright,
The sabre glitter to the sight,
Its splendor's lost, its polish vain,
Till some bold hand the steel sustain.

  Why have my days been stretch'd by fate,
To see the vile and vitious great,
While I, who led the race so long,
Am last and meanest of the throng?
Ah, why has death so long delay'd
To wrap me in his friendly shade,
Left me to wander thus alone,
When all my heart held dear is gone?

But let me check these fretful sighs —
Well may the base above me rise,
When yonder planets as they run
Mount in the sky above the sun.
Resign'd I bow to Fate's decree,
Nor hope his laws will change for me;
Each shifting scene, each varying hour,
But proves the ruthless tyrant's power.

But tho' with ills unnumber'd curst,
We owe to faithless man the worst;
For man can smile with specious art,
And plant a dagger in the heart.
He only's fitted for the strife
Which fills the boist'rous paths of life,
Who as he threads the crouded scenes
Upon no kindred bosom leans.
Too long my foolish heart had deem'd
Mankind as virtuous as they seem'd;

The spell is broke, their faults are bare,
And now I see them as they are;
Truth from each tainted breast has flown,
And falshood marks them all her own.
Incredulous I listen now
To every tongue, and every vow,
For still there yawns a gulph between
Those honied words, and what they mean;
With honest pride elate, I see
The sons of falshood shrink from me,
As from the right line's even way
The biass'd curves deflecting stray —
But what avails it to complain? —
With souls like theirs reproof is vain;
If honour e'er such bosoms share,
The sabre's point must fix it there.

But why exhaust life's vapid bowl,
And suck the dregs with sorrow foul,

When long ere this my youth has drain'd
Whatever zest the cup contain'd?
Why should we mount upon the wave,
And ocean's yawning horrors brave,
When we may swallow from the flask
Whate'er the wants of mortals ask?

Contentment's realms no fears invade,
No cares annoy, no sorrows shade,
There plac'd secure, in peace we rest,
Nor aught demand to make us blest.
While pleasure's gay fantastic bower,
The splendid pageant of an hour,
Like yonder meteor in the skies,
Flits with a breath no more to rise.

As thro' life's various walks we're led,
May prudence hover o'er our head!

May she our words, our actions guide,
Our faults correct, our secrets hide!
May she, where'er our footsteps stray,
Direct our paths, and clear the way!
Till, every scene of tumult past,
She bring us to repose at last,
Teach us to love that peaceful shore,
And roam thro' folly's wilds no more!

## LIV.

## TO YOUTH,

BY

## EBN ALRABIA, IN HIS OLD AGE.

Yes, youth, thou'rt fled, and I am left,
  Like yonder desolated bower,
By winter's ruthless hand bereft
  Of every leaf and every flower.

With heaving heart and streaming eyes
  I woo'd thee to prolong thy stay,
But vain were all my tears and sighs,
  Thou only fled'st more fast away.

Yet tho' thou fled'st away so fast,
    I can recall thee if I will;
For I can talk of what is past,
    And while I talk, enjoy thee still.

## LV.

## ON LOVE,

BY

## ABOU ALY, THE MATHEMATICIAN.

*ABOU ALY flourished in Egypt about the year* 530, *and was equally celebrated as a mathematician and as a poet.*

*In the following odd composition he seems to have united these two discordant characters.*

I NEVER knew a sprightly fair
 That was not dear to me,
And freely I my heart could share,
 With every one I see.

It is not *this* or *that* alone
   On whom my choice would fall,
I do not more incline to one
   Than I incline to all.

The circle's bounding line are they,
   Its center is my heart,
My ready love the equal ray
   That flows to every part.

## LXVI.

A
REMONSTRANCE WITH A DRUNKARD,
BY
YAHIA BEN SALAMET.

*THIS author was a native of Syria, and died at Miafarakir in the year of the Hejra* 553.

As drench'd in wine, the other night,
   Zeid from the banquet sallied,
Thus I reprov'd his drunken plight,
   Thus he my prudence rallied;

" In bev'rage so *impure* and *vile*,
   How canst thou thus delight?"—
" My cups," he answer'd with a smile,
   " Are generous and bright."

"Beware those dang'rous draughts," I cried,
  "With *love* the goblet flows"—
"And curst is he," the youth replied,
  "Who *hatred* only knows."

"Those cups too soon with sickness fraught
  Thy stomach shall deplore"—
"Then soon," he cried, "the noxious draught
  And all its ills are o'er."

"Rash youth, thy guilty joys resign"—
  "I will," at length he said,
"I vow I'll bid adieu to wine
  As soon as I am dead."

# LVII.

### VERSES ADDRESSED BY THE KHALIPH ALMOKTOFI LIAMRILLAH TO A LADY, WHO PRETENDED A PASSION FOR HIM IN HIS OLD AGE.

*ALMOKTOFI was the thirty-first Khaliph of the house of Abbas, and the only one who possessed any real authority since the reign of Radhi.*

*He was raised to the throne of the Khaliphs, upon the deposition of his nephew, by the influence, or rather appointment of the Seljuk Sultan Massoud. During the lifetime of his patron, Almoktofi continued, like his predecessors, in humble subjection to the will of the Sultan; but upon the death of Massoud he asserted his independence, and, after a short struggle, remained sole master of the city of Bagdad and the province of Mesopotamia. He died A. H. 555, having presided over the Khaliphat twenty-four years.*

*While the Khaliphs remained in a state of humiliation and dependence, they were either too much depressed to employ themselves in literature, or what is more probable, were too insignificant to have their employment attended to.*

*No compositions, at least by any of the Commanders of the Faithful, between the time of Radhi and Almoctafi are handed down to us; it is even asserted by Abulfeda that Radhi was the last of the Abbassides who attempted poetry; but the following verses (preserved by an anonymous historian of Syria, whose work is in the public library at Cambridge) prove that this assertion is not entirely accurate, and that Almoktafi, together with the power of the ancient Khaliphs, seems to have been ambitious of acquiring also some portion of their poetical reputation.*

THO' such unbounded love you swear,
   'Tis only art I see;
Can I believe that one so fair
   Should ever doat on me?

Say that you hate, and freely shew
   That age displeases youth;
And I may love you when I know
   That you can tell the truth.

## LVIII.
### ON
# PROCRASTINATION,
### BY
## HEBAT ALLAH IBN ALTALMITH.

*ABOUT the close of the sixth century of the Mohammedan æra, there lived in the East three physicians, almost equally celebrated for their abilities. They were all surnamed Hebat Allah* [i. e. *the gift of God*] *and each professed a different religion, one being a Christian, one a Mohammedan, and the other a Jew. The first of these, the author of the following composition, was a native of Bagdad, and considered by his countrymen as the greatest ornament of the place. Nor, if we may credit the character given of him by Abulfaraj, does their opinion of his merit seem to have been overrated: for according to this author* " *the elegance of his manners equalled his learning, and the sweetness of his disposition was only exceeded by the sublimity of his genius.*"

Ibn Altalmith was a favourite with all the princes who flourished at Bagdad during his time, but with Almoktafi he lived as a friend; the Khaliph could never suffer a week to pass without an interview with Ibn Altalmith, and the philosopher at every visit was received with fresh demonstrations of his sovereign's affection.

Notwithstanding these honours, and the many temporal advantages which he doubtless might have obtained by becoming a proselyte to Mohammedanism, Ibn Altalmith continued till his death a sincere adherent to Christianity: and in such abhorrence did he hold any change of religion from interested motives, that when his friend Hebat Allah, the Jewish physician, professed himself a convert to Islamism, Ibn Altalmith refused to hear the reasons which he attempted to allege in excuse for his conversion, and reproached him in the following terms; "Like your fathers you have been a long time wandering in the desert, and when you come out, like them you are at a greater distance from your journey's end than before."

Ibn Altalmith died in the 560th. year of the Hejra, at the advanced age of one hundred. His dying words are preserved by Abulfaraj, and prove, at least, that his vivacity was unimpaired to the last. Ibn Altalmith, says the historian, was expiring when his son approached his bed, and inquired *"If there was any thing he wished for?"* *Upon which the old man in a faint voice exclaimed, " I only wish that I could wish for any thing."*

---

Youth is a drunken noisy hour,
　With every folly fraught;
But man, by age's chast'ning power,
　Is sober'd into thought.


Then we resolve our faults to shun,
　And shape our course anew;
But ere the wise reform's begun
　Life closes on our view.


The travellers thus who wildly roam,
　Or heedlessly delay,
Are left, when they should reach their home,
　Benighted on the way.

---

## LIX.

ON THE

### EARLY DEATH OF ABOU ALHASSAN ALY, SON TO THE KHALIPH ALNASSAR LEDIN ALLAH,

BY

CAMAL EDDIN BEN ALNABIT.

*ALNASSAR LEDIN ALLAH was the thirty-fourth Abasside Khaliph, and the last excepting three who enjoyed this splendid title, which was finally abolished by the Tartars in the year* 656.

*The young man whose death is here lamented was Alnassar's favourite son and intended successor; and if his character, as represented in history, be just, he well deserved the preference his father entertained for him; for he seems to have possessed every virtue and accomplishment which could endear a son or adorn a prince.*

*Upon the death of Abou Aly, the Khaliph was inconsolable; he could think only of the loss he had sustained,* and his sole remaining pleasure was to resort perpetually to the tomb of his son, where he shut himself up, and abandoned himself to the most extravagant expressions of sorrow. Nor were the inhabitants of Bagdad less affected with the death of the young prince: there was scarce a house in the city, we are told by an historian, which did not resound with lamentation, nor a countenance that was not depressed by grief.

Alnassar died A. H. 622, having survived his son ten years.

This production of Camal Eddin's is rather a collection of epigrams to illustrate the same idea, viz. that the most valuable things are the most transitory, than a connected composition: the several thoughts however have novelty to recommend them, and they are not destitute of poetical merit.

---

SOON hast thou run the race of life,
   Nor could our tears thy speed controul—
Still in the courser's gen'rous strife
   The best\* will soonest reach the goal.

\* Literally the *outrunner* of *the outrunners:* The Arabians are so extremely accurate in every thing which respects their horses, that they have invented appropriate names, in order to distinguish the several competitors

As laid upon his hand, Death views
  Pearls, stones and gems of every kind;
From out the heap he first will choose
  The most resplendent he can find.

Thy name, by every breath'd convey'd,
  Stretch'd o'er the globe its boundless flight;
Alas, in eve the length'ning shade
  But lengthens to be lost in night!

If gracious ALLAH bade thee close
  Thy youthful eyes so soon on day,
'Tis that he readiest welcomes those
  Who love him best and best obey.

in a horse-race, according to their respective merits. Thus, instead of designing the horses as we do, the first, the second, the third, &c. they call the foremost the *outrunner*, the second the *backpresser*, the third the *tranquillizer*, &c. These names, as far as to the eleventh, are given by Taurizi, in his commentary upon the Hamasa.

AMOUGEH.

## LX.

### THE INTERVIEW,

A SONG IN THE RHYTHM OF THE ORIGINAL,
WITH THE MUSIC ANNEXED.

*THE music to this little air was written down by a friend, from the singing of David Zamir, a native of Bugdad, who resided with the translator for some time at Cambridge, and to whose assistance he is principally indebted for any knowledge he may have acquired in Oriental literature.*

*The Arabic is printed in the manner Zamir wrote it, with long vowels in the place of vowel points, by which he meant to mark the syllables where the principal emphasis was to be laid.*

D<small>ARKNESS</small> clos'd around, loud the tempest drove,
When thro' yonder glen I saw my lover rove,
 Dearest youth!
Soon he reach'd our cot weary, wet and cold,
But warmth, wine and I, to cheer his spirits strove,
 Dearest youth!

How my love, cried I, durst thou hither stray
Thro' the gloom, nor fear the ghosts that haunt the grove?
    Dearest youth!
In this heart, said he, fear no seat can find,
When each thought is fill'd alone with thee and love.
    Dearest maid!

www.ingramcontent.com/pod-product-compliance
Lightning Source LLC
Chambersburg PA
CBHW032132230426
43672CB00011B/2308